From Tragedy to Trust
a Mother's Story

Toni Wilkes
with Lea Eppling

**From Tragedy to Trust
a Mother's Story**

by Toni Wilkes
with Lea Eppling

ISBN 978-1-939283-12-2

Printed in the United States of America

Scriptures are taken from the KING JAMES VERSION (KJV): KING JAMES VERSION, public domain.

Permissions granted to use lyrics from: FORGIVENESS
Words and Music by MATTHEW WEST Copyright © 2010 SONGS OF SOUTHSIDE INDEPENDENT MUSIC PUBLISHING, SONGS FOR DELANEY and EXTERNAL COMBUSTION MUSIC. All Rights on behalf of itself and SONGS FOR DELANEY Administered by SONGS OF SOUTHSIDE INDEPENDENT MUSIC PUBLISHING. All Rights Reserved. Used By Permission of ALFRED MUSIC and One77 Songs (ASCAP. Kobalt Songs Music Publishing (ASCAP)

Text Design by Debbie Patrick, www.debbiepatrick.com

Published by:
Basic Inspiration
182 Church Street
Cleveland, Georgia

Dedication

To my husband and children. You lived this story with me. You, too, were broken, devastated, and lost. Yet, you were willing to let me tell "our story," even knowing the pain that reliving it would bring. Thank you for supporting me in this act of obedience and love. May those who read this book be encouraged by the healing God has given us over time. I love you all with every fiber of my being.

Contents

From Tragedy to Trust — A Mother's Story

Prologue

It is an early fall day in the South. Even though the weather is still warm, a nice breeze is blowing. I think of one of my favorite songs – Louis Armstrong's "What a Wonderful World." But I cannot listen to it without crying now because it serves as a reminder of when my world was truly wonderful. To be fair, my life has been blessed beyond measure. I'm in my early 50s and in good health. My husband is as kind and supportive as any woman could dream, and our two young adult children are healthy and love the Lord.

As I struggle with normal mid-life issues, I ponder my progress thus far. Have I done enough to leave a lasting legacy? For what will I be most remembered when my time on Earth is finished? I know, deep thoughts for a lovely fall afternoon; but I ponder just the same. What happens to the Christian who really begins to grow? Does following Jesus down the narrow path automatically open up to beautiful meadows of wildflowers? Or can obedience to Christ lead believers down a more treacherous road – to tragedy? Although I spent my life on the narrow path, it became almost impossible to navigate in June of 2011. That's when our oldest child, Courtney, was taken from us. The purpose for writing my story is to help others who are traveling the road of heartbreaking tragedy. If my journey of despair, weak faith, and rediscovery can lead you to hope, then God gets the glory.

First, let me introduce you to my precious daughter Courtney. She came into this world with red hair and with the personality to go with it. She always knew what she liked and didn't like. She was stubborn without being strong willed. Even as a toddler, Courtney did not follow what the other children were doing. Because she was extremely quiet, she was often thought to be a loner. But those who knew Courtney best knew that she was simply an old soul. Looking back, I can see that she was wiser than her years and more grounded than some adults. Courtney was funny and bright with a quick smile, usually seeking out the underdogs to befriend. Courtney loved animals with a passion, which led to her dream of becoming a veterinarian. Even at 15 years of age, she was working towards that goal. She wasn't perfect by any means, and she did sometimes buck our rules. Still, Courtney was kind and observant of others' needs. She was a peacemaker with her siblings and an absolute joy to our lives. Yes, Courtney was a unique young lady. I have said on countless occasions that she was born to be a shooting star.

About a month after my daughter's funeral, God impressed upon my heart to write a book about the spiritual journey I was taking. It was a fleeting thought initially. And honestly, I wasn't keen on the idea at the time because my pain was still very raw. Even though I was journaling on a weekly basis, putting those real and personal thoughts out there for others to read did not appeal to me. Yet I could not shake the thought that this was exactly what God wanted me to do. Had I known then what an excruciating journey this would become, my resistance would have been even greater. I didn't begin this project for quite some time. Writing my story has required emotional and spiritual transparency, which has taken more courage than I knew I possessed. This book is not just my story of grief, my crisis of faith, or even my way to help others. What you are reading is an act of obedience to God. He has been very real to me throughout the loss of my child, as well as the loss of who I thought I was.

If you are in the midst of a life-shattering tragedy, then I highly recommend that you keep a Bible close at hand while reading this book. I pray that my story will give you hope in these dark days. But my story itself cannot change your life; it can only point you to the One who can. As you read, allow the principles from God's Word to penetrate deep into your heart. Please know that I am praying for you.

Chapter 1:
Overcoming Misconceptions

What do you think of when you hear the word "tragedy?" The picture that just came into your mind is most likely based on your life experiences. Not everyone will experience a tragedy. Some will experience multiple tragedies. Responding to any kind of life-changing heartache is a difficult process, even for people of faith. For me, the word tragedy will forever be associated with the sudden and brutal murder of my daughter, Courtney. Responding to her death in faith has been the struggle of a lifetime.

It's been over eight years since Courtney went to Heaven. During that time my faith has grown deeper and stronger than ever before. As I think back, I hardly recognize the woman I was before. This in no way minimizes the fact that our lives were shattered. The pain and heartache of my loss is never completely gone. What has changed is how I think and what I believe. Like the refiner's fire, God is using our tragedy to remove the dross in my life. He's helping me overcome the misconceptions I had about myself and about Him.

You see, I used to believe the Christian walk was smoother based on a believer's faithfulness. As long as I remained obedient to the Lord, then I thought my life would progress without significant hardship. I'm not sure at what point I adopted this view. It wasn't something I gleaned from reading the Bible. Nor was it something I was ever taught by my pastor, who also happened to be my father. He encouraged his congregation to dedicate their lives to serving Christ, but he certainly never preached that following Jesus was easy. Somehow, I just came to believe this was true. The fact that my life had been relatively trouble-free led me to think I was immune to this kind of heartache. My faith was rocked when I realized that this belief was just a misconception.

Growing up, I was not the stereotypical preacher's kid. I didn't resent the expectations that came with my father's calling. Instead, I assumed ownership of my faith at an early age. The fact that my behavior reflected on his ministry was a responsibility I took seriously. Even though I was a typical teenager in many ways, outright rebellion just never occurred to me. Then, while trying to cope with my grief, I began to wonder why I had steered clear of trouble all my life. Was it just because I had strict parents? Was it because I didn't want to disappoint them? Then a realization hit me. The motivating force of my life was trying to keep God from being mad at me. Of course, a desire to please God is good (1 Thessalonians 4:1). But my obedience was rooted more in fear of losing His blessings rather than rooted in love for Him.

My Christian life was built around passages describing the Lord's strong desire for His children to be faithful. For instance, in 2 Chronicles 19:9 Jehoshaphat charged the Levites, priests, and the chief of the fathers of Israel, *"Thus shall ye do in the fear of the Lord, faithfully, and with a perfect heart."* And 1 Corinthians 4:2, *"Moreover it is required in stewards, that a man be found faithful."* Why, then, did

He not stop the thing I feared the most from happening? Hadn't He said that those who live faithfully are His delight? How many times did I hear my father say that God puts His premium on faithfulness? The problem wasn't with God's Word, the problem was with my understanding of it.

Before Courtney's death, my Christian walk was built on me. My focus had always been on what I did, not on what God has done. I thought more about who I was rather than who God is. It was an "if, then" faith. If I just stayed as close to Christ as possible and tried to do right, then I thought God would keep trouble and tragedy out of my life. So, not only did my daughter's death shake my faith – the way she was taken from us contradicted my deepest held belief.

At my very weakest moments, I felt betrayed, as if the Lord had failed me and broken His promises. Because of these misconceived notions, our tragedy took a toll on my faith. Everything I thought and believed about God's goodness and faithfulness was in disarray. I vacillated between what I knew to be true and what I suddenly questioned.

There was never a doubt about my salvation; it was firmly intact. I loved God and wanted to serve Him however I could. I just didn't trust Him anymore. If you've never been in the depths of despair, then that probably doesn't make sense to you. Yet, it is exactly where I was spiritually. Even now, I'm ashamed to say it out loud. How could I not trust the One who created me? How could I doubt that the One who didn't spare His own Son to save me, truly loved me? But I did doubt it.

Of course, there's actually plenty of biblical evidence for suffering in the lives of God's faithful servants. The Bible tells of people who served God with their entire being and still faced terrifying and life-changing struggles. For instance, Jeremiah faithfully preached the Lord's message to Israel, despite enduring abuse for his obedience. It's easy to understand why he's called the "weeping prophet." Eventually, he was stoned to death by the very people over whom he wept. I've wrestled with studying the life of Job, who suffered unimaginable loss. God gave permission for Job to lose everything, including all of his children, even though God called him "My servant." His struggle with the Lord is transparent, which I can now appreciate. Still, Job proclaims, *"Though He slay me, yet will I trust in Him"* (Job 13:15). It has taken me years to wrap my mind around those ten words. Many others in the Bible served faithfully, regardless of whether or not the outcome was what they had hoped. Despite having heard and believed these stories all of my life, I had somehow separated these biblical accounts from my reality.

During my initial days of grief, I experienced such heart-rending confusion and sadness that to this day I cannot talk about it. I mourned terribly, not just for Courtney, but for my old life. It's difficult to describe the feeling of doubting the Lord's love and kindness, yet, at the same time, knowing that He was my only hope of surviving the overwhelming grief. So, I turned to Scripture. And God faithfully spoke to my aching heart throughout my time of doubt. As I sought answers in God's Word, He provided comfort and hope by correcting my misconceptions.

Misconception: My faithfulness to God makes me immune from heartbreak.

Correcting this misconception was foundational to strengthening my faith. During this time, a familiar passage seemed to leap from the pages of my Bible and speak directly to me, *"These things I have spoken unto you, that in me ye might have peace. In the world ye shall have tribulation: but be of good cheer; I have overcome the world"* (John 16:33). Although I knew this verse well, my definition of life's troubles and tribulations never included this kind of life-shattering tragedy. In actuality, that's exactly what Jesus is talking about just a few verses earlier. He predicts His own cruel death and the grief that would engulf those closest to Him. The very ones who gave up everything to follow Him were not immune to heartbreak. And what about Mary? I think about her standing before the Cross, watching her son's crucifixion. Her heartache and grief are unimaginable to me.

As His followers today, Jesus forewarns us that troubles and tribulation are a reality of living in this sinful world. It is not a matter of *if*, but *when*. What I believed about God and Christian suffering was completely wrong. My misunderstanding was not God's deceit. My idea that I was immune from tragedy was simply that – my idea! The Lord never promises any believer an easy life. Therefore, He did not lie to me or mislead me.

There is a connection between our faithfulness to God and His faithfulness to us, but it's not an "if, then" correlation. The Lord remains faithful to His children, even when the world gives us its worst. Now, I have a new understanding of verses such as Lamentations 3:22, *"It is of the Lord's mercies that we are not consumed, because his compassions fail not. They are new every morning: great is thy faithfulness."* And, I can say with the psalmist, *"I will sing of the mercies of the Lord forever: with my mouth will I make known thy faithfulness to all generations"* (Psalm 89:1).

A Glimmer of Hope

Even when my mind started coming to grips with the truth, my heart did not. A feeling of hopelessness covered me like a blanket. I was weary and weak – mentally, emotionally, and spiritually. Hope is an interesting thing. It's the light at the end of the dark tunnel that keeps the human spirit strong. Whereas hopelessness can make it seem physically impossible to get out of bed. So again, I opened my Bible and turned to the only One who knew me completely and understood the state I was in.

Isaiah 40:27-30 describes those who lack courage and strength as *"the faint."* I thought, "Well, at least I finally have a name for my stumbling faith." In those same verses, Isaiah reminds Israel that God sees and understands their situation in its entirety. And He never grows tired or weary. He *"fainteth not."* The Lord Himself was their hope.

Then, Isaiah uses the plight of the eagle to encourage those who are faint of heart. You see, eagles go through a molting process before experiencing a rebirth, of sorts. During this period, each eagle must decide if he is going to live or die. Those who wait the process out, emerge mature and stronger than before. Isaiah 40:31 describes the analogy beautifully, *"But they that wait upon the Lord shall renew their strength; they shall mount up with wings as eagles; they shall run, and not be weary; and they shall walk, and not faint."*

The Lord was meeting me exactly where I was. I'd like to tell you that my doubt miraculously vanished in that moment; it did not. While I couldn't imagine having that kind of strength, Isaiah's words were the glimmer of hope I needed to keep trudging through this dark tunnel.

Misconception: My faith is strong.

Overcoming my misconceptions about God and about my faith was a long process. I was naïve, however, about the path the process needed to take, and I was still naïve about myself. Prior to June of 2011, I thought my faith was strong. In actuality, it had never been tried or tested. Looking back, I had a "milk baby" faith at best. I

Corinthians 4:1-2 was convicting, *"And I, brethren, could not speak unto you as unto spiritual, but as unto carnal, even as unto babes in Christ. I have fed you with milk, and not with meat: for hitherto ye were not able to bear it, neither yet now are ye able."*

The very thought that my faith was somehow immature was a blow, even though there was evidence it was true. For instance, when I was initially offered counseling, I turned it down. "After all," I thought, "I'm a pastor's daughter. I grew up in church. I know what the Bible says and where to turn in Scripture to find what I need." At the time, I didn't understand that His comfort and guidance can come in many forms, including Christian counseling. Although I was clinging to the words of Isaiah, determined to *"wait upon the Lord,"* I had to overcome the idea that being tough was the same as having mature faith.

The apostle Paul certainly understood this truth when he wrote, *"Therefore I take pleasure in infirmities, in reproaches, in necessities, in persecutions, in distresses for Christ's sake: for when I am weak, then am I strong"* (2 Corinthians 12:10). This principle now rings true for me. What I thought was strength was actually a form of arrogance. By refusing professional counseling, I had unintentionally pushed away God's effort to help me, which caused additional struggle. At my lowest moment I had no choice but to humbly admit my weakness and accept the help I needed. In order to live in the strength of Christ, I had to die to the idea of living in my own strength and to my determination to appear strong.

Of course, I already felt like I died right along with Courtney that night. Any parent who experiences the loss of a child understands that part of their heart dies as well. In Scripture, however, Paul was referring to a spiritual death when he said, *"I die daily"* (I Corinthians 15:31). Based on this verse, I've heard preachers suggest that we look in the mirror each morning and tell the reflection, "You are dead." While this may seem silly, it certainly drives home the point. I could not become dependent upon God without first completely surrendering to Him. This required dying to myself. John 12:24 reminds us that a seed must die in order to live, *"Verily, verily, I say unto you, except a corn of wheat fall into the ground and die, it abideth alone: but if it die, it bringeth forth much fruit."* I was that corn of wheat. I had to die in order to become what God intended for me to be as His child. What little faith I had needed to be offered up to my heavenly Father. Only then could it grow into something beautiful for Christ.

In one way or another, all believers are faced with the realization that we don't have the answers. In that moment, we must each decide where to turn. If our faith, however weak it may be, is grounded in the truth of Scripture, then we turn to Christ. He continues to prove that He is all the strength I need.

Misconception: I know who God is.

I'm convinced that this misconception is quite common among believers. We tend to define God by latching on to one or two of His characteristics. Many Christians stop at the words, "God is love" or "God is holy." So, our faith can flounder when circumstances come about in our lives that don't seem to reflect how we view God. In reality, the depth and breadth of God's character cannot be fully realized, even in a lifetime of faithful service. I had always reverenced God, but my grief fueled the desire to know Him on a deeper level.

Over the years since Courtney's death, I've discovered that suffering allows us to go deeper with God. My heart wrestled with the concept in Philippians 3:10, *"That I may know Him and the power of His resurrection and the fellowship of His sufferings, being made conformable unto His death."* This particular verse both touched and tore at my heart. Did I really have to experience such heart-wrenching pain in order to know God better? The enemy began working overtime on my mind. Why would the Lord allow me to hurt so badly if He truly loved me? Then I was reminded that Jesus willingly went to the Cross, which boggles my mind. He bore the vilest of sins, including the very evil that shattered my life. Evil will not have the final word.

Of course, no suffering we experience truly compares to His. Yet, through the fellowship of suffering, we are privileged to know Him in a way that many people never will. God came to me in the midst of my heartache. He was there, without fail, when I thought I'd never smile again. While He restored my ability to smile, it's a different smile now. It's the result of peace birthed through intense pain and heartache. The kind of peace that only comes from truly knowing the One who has *"overcome the world"* (John 16:33).

Do you have similar misconceptions about God and about your faith? If you're struggling with why a good and loving God allows such evil, then keep reading. But please let this thought wash over you before you turn the page: God's Word is what corrected my misconceived notions. Digging deeply into Scripture gave me hope, courage, and peace. It's how I learned to trust Him with my tragedy. No matter what tribulation you are currently suffering, His strength will eventually lift you out of the pit…if you will seek Him. Now, I'd like to share my story with you.

Chapter 2:
The Storm Strikes

Every story has a beginning. My story begins on Monday, June 13, 2011. It was the first day of summer vacation at our favorite beach destination – Seagrove Beach near Panama City, Florida. We've always enjoyed long family vacations to places that keep us on the go. I have such wonderful memories of summers at Yellowstone National Park, the Grand Canyon, Mount Rushmore, and the Smoky Mountains. But in the summer of 2011, Cordy and I decided to take a more relaxing vacation. Maybe the stage we were in as a family factored into the decision. Our oldest daughter, Courtney, was turning sixteen in three weeks. So, we were mentally preparing for all the challenges that come with a dating and driving teenage daughter. And our other two children were not too far behind her (Callie was 14 and Cole was 11.) As I stood at the window of our condominium, looking out over our view of the beach, I envisioned a week of fun, but mostly a week of relaxation.

Later that day, the girls and I made use of the chairs on the beach. We noticed two young men removing and stacking chairs near the boardwalk. The younger boy came over and said we could stay in the chairs for a while, but a storm was coming and the weather would soon force us off the beach. The girls, being teenagers, were giddy when he offered us a few sand dollars. Looking back, I see both the significance and the irony of that encounter. Yes, a storm was brewing offshore, but the storm brewing inside that young man would be far more damaging to our family.

We assumed the two boys were employed by either the condominium owners or the city. More information came to light over the next few days. They were brothers. The older one worked for the condominiums, but the younger one (who spoke to us) was just hanging out. The younger brother had been asked not to come around because he distracted his brother from work. It was discovered later that he was living in a campsite not far from the beach; his parents had recently kicked him out of the house. Of course, we were completely unaware of the dangerous forces inside him that day on the beach. All this information came far too late for us. He just seemed to be a nice, innocent young man. So, we had no uneasy feelings or fears as we relaxed on the beach, talking about the fun we were going to have that week.

We went to the beach early the next morning to secure a location near the water. The chairs hadn't even been set out when we arrived. The older brother was in the process of getting them out and asked if any of the kids wanted to make a little cash and help. Courtney quickly volunteered while the other two headed to the water. Cordy and I kept an eye on her the entire time but had no real reason for concern. We did typical beach things over the next few days – went for walks, read, sunbathed, and played in the surf. During that time, we had a few conversations with the younger brother. He was friendly when we asked a few general questions about the area and about himself.

On Thursday, we planned to leave the beach early in the afternoon to go into town and shop. Courtney approached us after lunch and said that the younger of the two brothers, who she referred to as the "lifeguard dude," had asked if she could go for a walk. Although we were a little hesitant, we knew she would soon be dating. And after all, it was just a walk. So after instructing her to be responsible, we allowed her to go. We had no idea that was our last conversation with Courtney. We never saw her alive again.

After about 45 minutes, Cordy and I became increasingly uneasy. We decided to give her ten more minutes then go looking for her. When she didn't arrive, all four of us headed down the beach in the direction we had watched her go. After walking for a while, we sent Callie and Cole back to the area on the beach where we were camped out, in case Courtney was looking for us there. We combed the beach in both directions with no sign of her. After three miles we decided to turn back. I remember asking Cordy if we should be worried. He kept saying, "Not yet." But when we got back to Callie and Cole, and Courtney hadn't returned, Cordy said, "Now we worry."

We called 911. I remember repeatedly saying, "I'm the worst mother ever." We gave the authorities the details, and they sent the fire department out to search the beach. One moment in particular stands out from that afternoon. When the police questioned the older brother, I looked him straight in the eyes and asked if his brother would hurt Courtney. He hesitated a bit too long before saying, "No." Cordy went with officers to help with the search while I went back to the condominium with Callie and Cole.

Each hour of waiting was excruciating. I had no concept of time. In reality, it was about four hours of filling out forms, starting prayer chains, and pacing…lots of pacing. One of the few comforts during those hours was a phone call with my father. He had a peace in his heart that she was going to be okay. It wasn't until much later that we realized he was right; it was just a different kind of okay than we were praying for.

No matter how long I live, I'll never forget the moment Cordy returned, accompanied by two deputies. This moment is forever seared on my mind. He was visibly shaken, white in the face, and his hands were stretched out toward me. It felt like we were moving in slow motion. My ears were ringing; I felt sick as Cordy said, "They found her. It's not good...he killed her."

I immediately started screaming, ran to the other room, and threw myself on the bed. In those first moments, thoughts couldn't form – only reactions. I'm not sure what a good reaction would have been, or even if one exists. In my distraught state, I ran to the balcony and picked up a chair with the intention of throwing it off. But then good sense (or the Holy Spirit) prevailed. One thought finally took over, "We need to pray." So, I grabbed Cordy and the kids; we fell to our knees in front of the couch, almost in unison. We begged the Lord for help and assured one another that this tragedy would not tear our family apart.

I only made three calls after we got the news – my father and two close friends. When I called my parents, all I could say at first was, "Daddy." Hearing my mother break down was so hard. Cordy called Courtney's godfather who drove to break the news to my in-laws. We began receiving phone calls almost immediately. Even seven hours away from home, we were blessed with friends and beautiful souls who wanted to help. People contacted us non-stop all night. Texts came in every few minutes. The Florida authorities left for the night but didn't go far. A local pastor came by to offer what comfort he could. And one of Callie's high school friends, who happened to be in the area, came to comfort her. I remember just wanting my daddy. Our families were on the way, but it seemed like an eternity before they finally arrived.

So, we waited, clinging to our sanity. We were all in shock; we just didn't recognize it at the time. It's almost impossible to convey the emotions of those first hours. Each of us responded differently. Cole cried inconsolably for a long time. After talking to a local pastor, he finally calmed down and drifted off to sleep. We were grateful he had momentary relief from the grief. Callie, on the other hand, was quiet. By nature, she has a positive personality and looks for the good in any situation, which was impossible that night. I've come to believe that she was angry beyond expression. So rather than adding to our sorrow by lashing out, she chose to shut down. Cordy busied himself by packing Courtney's belongings. I had rarely, if ever, seen my husband cry. That day, however, He cried in a way I've never heard anyone cry before. Even now, just thinking about the sound of his crying takes me back to those first hours. Words fail to describe how it feels to have your heart ripped from your chest. But the sound of my husband's grief spilling from that bedroom encompassed it completely.

I didn't know what to do. I would sit, then lie down, then walk around. Because of the shock, I was alternately numb and then shaking. Time was still moving in slow motion. For some reason, sitting quietly and listening to the tick-tock of the clock was oddly comforting. I felt disconnected from my own body, as if I had faded away from sheer sadness. If God had given me the option of simply disappearing, I would have taken it. I needed relief from one recurring thought: how could I have allowed this to happen?

At some point, Cordy and I walked out to the place on the beach where we had last seen Courtney. The moon was red and full. Memories from the night before came flooding back. We had gone to an outdoor concert and walked back on the beach. As Courtney and Cole walked near the surf, she said, "This must be what everyone means by taking a moonlit walk on the beach. But what a waste to do it with my brother!" Of course, we all laughed. Now, under that same full moon, we told Courtney goodbye. I remember thinking it was the saddest moon I'd ever seen.

Our entire family arrived before dawn. Grandparents, aunts, uncles, and godparents all came. We've always had a good family support system, but we didn't know how strong it actually was. In the weeks, months, and years that followed, our family shored us up. They took care of us in every way you can imagine. As that long night turned into morning, they sat and cried with us. Even though no words could diminish our pain, their presence brought me strength. Simply put – they were there. While we were talking, the sun came up as if nothing had happened. It was hard to believe the world hadn't stopped turning.

Like the day we arrived, I looked out over our view of the beach. But this time it was different; I was different. We never saw the storm brewing inside that young man, yet it struck our family with unimaginable devastation. The events of that day, combined with my misconceptions about God, created the conditions for a perfect storm. I was about to suffer a crisis of faith.

Chapter 3:
Completely Overwhelmed

Those first days after losing Courtney were overwhelming. That word kept coming up… overwhelmed. It was as if a tidal wave of grief and grace engulfed me continually. The pain was almost unbearable, yet there was a constant awareness of God's presence. I remember feeling like my feet weren't touching the ground. While I recognized God's hand at the time, I didn't realize just how important this flood of grace would be later on. God would soon have to remind me of how His grace carried me through, especially that first week. Because God's grace is multi-faceted, it comes in many forms; and because it's immeasurable, His grace never runs dry. In the days immediately following Courtney's death, His grace came through the kindness and compassion of loving family, old friends, and people we had just met.

Calls from home were coming at an almost unmanageable rate as word spread. People were praying. The authorities in Florida prepared us to stay for several days since the autopsy and crime scene evaluation could take quite some time. We were given a more private place to stay (away from the media) and provided with food. People came and went. We were learning more about exactly what had happened but were also being shielded from specific details. The investigators were very careful about what information they shared and how they shared it. Even that was God taking care of us – not giving us more than we could handle at the time. Being so far from home left us feeling somewhat helpless. But every official – from the fire department workers who responded initially, to the officers who combed the beach, to the lead detectives who worked the crime scene – went over and above their job duties. I truly believe God worked through them on our behalf. Each person involved seemed to take our loss personally. Courtney wasn't just a victim; she could have been their daughter, granddaughter, niece, sister, or friend. They worked with a sense of urgency to ensure we wouldn't be required to stay longer than need be. Even the doctor who performed the autopsy communicated with Cordy personally, keeping us updated.

So, by late Friday afternoon, we were on our way to Pensacola to meet up with the van transporting Courtney home. It was the saddest and quietest ride I can ever remember. I still hadn't eaten and had gotten only short moments of sleep. On the way home, instead of reminiscing about a wonderful vacation, we planned Courtney's funeral and talked about where we would lay her to rest. We planned to take Courtney to the funeral home as soon as we arrived, but Cole protested. He wanted to take her home first. So, our convoy pulled into the yard in the wee hours of the morning on June 18, 2011. Cordy opened the back door of the van, touched Courtney's toe, and told her she was home. We unloaded her bags and put them on her bed. It would be several weeks before they were unpacked.

Overwhelming Support

When we finally took Courtney to the funeral home, the director was waiting for us. Apparently, the response had already been so large that he didn't think they could accommodate the visitation or the funeral. So, a large local church offered their facilities. Plans needed to be made of course. Yet, my biggest concern at that moment was that Courtney not be alone. Looking back, I know it was an unreasonable request but every fiber of my being was still trying to protect her. The director assured us that they would not leave our baby alone for even a minute. With that small comfort, we headed back home. Exhausted and numb, we fell into our beds. I felt the presence of ministering angels as I finally went to sleep. It took me a few minutes the next morning to realize that it wasn't all a bad dream; which was something that happened every morning for a long time. In the days and weeks that followed, I looked forward to going to bed because it was the only time I could escape this new reality.

The first day home was consumed with funeral arrangements and friends. My mind shifted between grieving mother and fretting hostess. I remember suddenly thinking, "It's a summer day, and I don't have anything for people to drink!" But of course, enough had already been brought. In my state of mind, I just wasn't fully aware of everything happening around me. Cordy made himself busy, which has always been his way. A friend helped him get the house ready for guests. People started coming about mid-morning with more food, hugs, and encouragement. I went through the motions, trying to be brave and putting on a good front. The reasonable part of my mind truly appreciated everyone who came, but the other part of me just wanted to be left alone. Although it was difficult, engaging every guest and speaking with every person who called occupied my mind for a time. It was late into the night when the last person finally hugged us goodbye, and we were alone again. But the empty house I longed for earlier in the day was extremely quiet when they left - too quiet. As soon as the door closed, I wanted them all to come back. My life was so out of control that I controlled the only thing I could – my house. So, I got busy cleaning. Cordy forced me to stop by prying the vacuum cleaner from my hands. It was actually a welcomed relief when he convinced me it was time to go to bed. Somehow, God graciously quieted my mind, allowing me to sleep peacefully through the night.

The next day was Father's Day, which instantly became my least favorite holiday. It was too much to face so soon after the loss of our first child. None of the fathers in our family wanted to celebrate, so we bunkered down at the house. I was told later that our church service was completely full. People came to show their support for our family and to pray for us. Again, we received friends at the house for the better part of the day. By this time, we had so much food that we could have fed any number of guests. Even though Cordy and I had no appetite, it was nice that our friends and church family took care of the basics so we could simply be present. It amazes me that Christian fellowship seems sweetest at times like these. Just when the grief seemed too much to bear, a brother or sister in Christ was there to cry with us. They also reminisced with us by looking through my scrapbooks. Pictures sparked sweet memories of our incredible daughter. There were even brief moments of laughter when a funny story about Courtney was told. I had to excuse myself a couple of times to cry. But after a few minutes, I pulled myself together and went back out to join everyone. God's grace was holding me every minute.

The next morning, we headed to the funeral home to finalize the arrangements. As we pulled into town, we were overwhelmed by what we saw. White bows seemed to be placed on every immovable object – and even some moveable ones. Almost every business had a message on their sign, "Pray for the Wilkes family," "Remembering Courtney," "Love Bears All Things," and many other sweet words of encouragement. These words were a healing balm to my mind, which was full of guilt for not stopping what had happened in the first place. My expectation was to be judged as a bad parent, but now I knew that our community loved us and was grieving with us. Putting their love into action gave us the boost we needed to accomplish what would otherwise have been too much for us. Even more, I felt their prayers. It gave me the strength to get out of the car and walk inside. It amazes me that we had the clarity of mind to make the funeral arrangements – from pall bearers to music to the program. Some of these details had been discussed in our few moments of clarity on the ride home from Florida. Other details simply fell into place when we needed them. The only explanation is that this tidal wave of grief was continually balanced with God's grace.

At our request, the funeral director checked on the legalities of burying Courtney at home on our farm, an idea that originated on that long drive home from Florida. Courtney loved our home and always seemed happiest when she was there. Cordy picked out a location on our property and I agreed. I wanted her close where we could look after her. The director told us we were cleared. There was no reason why we couldn't bury Courtney exactly where we wished. He also reminded us that he anticipated a large showing for visitation the next day. So, we would need to begin early and be prepared to stay for a while. I still had not seen Courtney. Just thinking about that moment made me physically sick. It was coming, nonetheless. But God would supply strength for the next day, just as He had been doing.

Several months earlier, Courtney and I had started making "bucket lists" just for fun. I loved hearing the things she wanted to do and places she wanted to see. We actually talked about it a little the night before she died. It's funny how those little conversations seem monumental now. Anyway, one of the items on her list was rather strange. For some reason she thought going through a drive-thru backwards would be hilarious. So after making the arrangements for the funeral, Cordy decided to cross one item off her list. As we pulled into Sonic to get drinks, he suddenly backed the car up and pulled out of line. Callie quickly figured it out and said, "Oh Daddy!" Now, the Sonic drive-thru is tricky. It curves and the curbs are weird. Still, he maneuvered it like an obstacle course. When we pulled up to the window to pay, the look on the cashier's face was priceless. Of course, we explained what we were doing. By the time we left, not only were we crying but so were all the employees. Such moments were like release valves on a pressure cooker. The pure silliness made us all smile, even through the tears.

When we finally arrived back home, we were overwhelmed once again. One of our dear friends had arranged to clear a whole section of trees so we'd be able to see Courtney's burial place from the house. Another troop of volunteers moved fences to keep our cows away from that location. We wanted to eventually make "Courtney's Place" a retreat of sorts – a dream which came true much earlier than planned.

The visits, calls, and cards continued to come in droves, as did social media posts from all over the country. In the small town of Seagrove, Florida, where Courtney was murdered, people put white bows on their mailboxes and sent cards and flowers. The way in which Courtney died was a huge part of the outpouring. But the love and support from that community was so genuine… it left us speechless.

We have no idea how many visitors we had during those days. We just know it was in the hundreds. Family and friends came from all over. So, I enlisted help to keep up with the food and gifts that were brought. Not one person actually expected a thank you note, but thinking about those kinds of things kept my mind busy. Friends helped with cleaning the kitchen, answering the phone, and doing the laundry. Families were also taking care of my kids, keeping their minds occupied. Callie was whisked away to swim or shop, and Cole's friends came to the house. A few close friends even went shopping and brought back piles of clothes so I would have choices for the visitation and the funeral. Imagine my surprise when I was able to laugh a little during a mini-fashion show as they helped me decide what was most appropriate to wear. At a tremendously difficult moment, those women were God's hands and feet. I'd heard people talk about distinctly experiencing the grace of God during times of great distress; but now it's real to me. The Lord knew how desperately I needed His grace the next day, as I put those clothes on and prepared for Courtney's visitation.

Overwhelming Sorrow

Even now, that day remains vivid in my memory. I awoke both physically and emotionally sick. The day I dreaded had arrived. Not only would we see Courtney for the first time, but we would also have to face the community as a whole. Although we'd experienced overwhelming support, we were also riddled with guilt for allowing Courtney to walk off that day. We felt like horrible parents. We should have somehow seen the evil behind his eyes. We should have asked more questions. If we were thinking this, certainly others were as well. So, we didn't really know what to expect. But we learned very quickly that our precious friends and loved ones never looked at it that way. They simply wanted us to know that they were there. We knew we were in for a long day as we left the house. Still, nothing could have truly prepared us for what that day brought.

Only one word describes how I felt as we arrived at the funeral home – terror. Cordy and I wanted to see Courtney first because we hadn't decided whether the casket would be opened or closed. We just didn't know how much she would look like our Courtney. So, we walked what felt like the *Green Mile* to where she lay. We had chosen a beautiful blue casket. It was her favorite color. As we approached, my heart seemed to stop. I've never felt such overwhelming sorrow. There in that lovely box lay my heart. We knew immediately that we would not allow the kids to see Courtney; nor did we want our friends in the community to remember her that way. As parents, we wanted Callie and Cole to remember the image of Courtney they held in their hearts. They understood and were somewhat relieved, I think. We did bring in immediate family members who wanted to say goodbye. It was an unforgettably heartbreaking moment for us all. Cordy and I were the last ones to see her before the casket closed. Goodbye seems so trite. In a moment like that, what do you say or do? How do you tell her you're sorry that you didn't protect her better? How do you close the lid and walk away from your hopes and dreams? How do you look at your baby for the last time on this earth and not die yourself? My only answer then – and still to this day – is that you hold your arms up like a small child and ask your heavenly Father to pick you up and hold you. After regaining our composure, we left for the public visitation at the church.

I can still imagine that scene in my mind's eye. I'd never seen that many flowers and plants in one location. Tokens of love and respect blanketed the entire front of the sanctuary. At the front, as the centerpiece of that arrangement, was our baby; with her beautiful portrait placed beside the casket. In the corner, a DVD with pictures of Courtney's life played in a loop. The music from the DVD drifted through the air like a soundtrack for the entire day. As we positioned ourselves to receive visitors, we took a few very deep breaths. Close friends stayed nearby to assure we weren't inundated with too many people at one time. However, there was not a lull for the next six hours. People came out in droves to show their support. To this day we have no idea how many actually came. The line to sign the visitor's book was so long that many people couldn't wait. But even if their names aren't written down, I remember the sea of faces from every part of our lives: family, friends, co-workers, church members, and many mere acquaintances. We were given hugs, books, and commemorative buttons. It's strange, but I don't recall many tears; a sure sign that God's grace was holding us together. As a matter of fact, about half-way through the night we found ourselves comforting others. We were surviving.

A thought occurred to me in the weeks that followed. Courtney was to turn sixteen on July 9th. We'd discussed various options for a "sweet sixteen" party, but not liking the spotlight, Courtney never committed to a party. She didn't think anyone would come, especially with it being in the summer. So, as I thought about the number of people who came to show their respect and love for her, it was the very definition of irony. She never knew how many lives she was touching in her own short life. How many people live their entire lives without knowing the impact they've had on others? Our community had noticed Courtney's godly character. And we were grateful.

Overwhelming Grace

The morning of Courtney's funeral arrived. Even though it would be the hardest day of my life, I wanted to remember everything;

and I do. Not one detail of that day has diminished in my mind. It was very hot, as it typically is in late June in South Georgia. Even more flowers and arrangements had been placed at the church. Friends and family were already waiting in our holding room. We saw family we hadn't seen in years. And our church family had been right beside us during the entire ordeal. What brought the most emotion, though, was seeing the officers and deputies from Florida who drove up for the day. As we waited to begin the ceremony, people came in to pray with us or simply to offer a hug. Looking around at all the people who were there for us and for Courtney, I was once again overwhelmed.

My mind drifted to a conversation a few days before. My father and I were sitting in the living room discussing the funeral, which he was to preach – a decision made on the way home from Florida. Daddy didn't want to preach the funeral, but we all knew that Courtney would have it no other way. He was the only one who could say what needed to be said. Still, it would be the hardest funeral he ever preached, and he was experiencing a total mental block. How do you talk about a life full of love and laughter taken too soon, especially when that young life was part of you? This day was our one opportunity to speak to our friends, extended family, and community about Courtney. We had to do it right. So, as we were talking, he asked for her Bible. After I retrieved it, he found a Sunday school lesson from the previous week nestled in the book of Joshua. Verse 1:9 was highlighted, *"Have not I commanded you. Be strong and of a good courage; Be not afraid, neither be thou dismayed: for the Lord thy God is with thee whithersoever thou goest."* Suddenly, he looked at me, "She's preaching her own funeral." He had his sermon from that verse and that Sunday school lesson. It was just one of many times over the next few months that we would experience the overwhelming grace of God.

So, we stood in that room, waiting. We waited for healing. We waited for closure. We waited for answers. Many of which we still don't have and probably never will. But God's grace was present in abundance. We were being held and carried along. The time finally arrived. We lined up to go inside, knowing we were not in any way prepared for this moment. I felt numb and peaceful at the same time. In one hand was a stuffed bear, a gift from one of the deputies. The other hand clung tightly to Cordy's. As we entered the church, we felt the love and support of our community in a huge way. That large auditorium was full-to-capacity. I immediately began to weep.

The service opened with one of Courtney's favorite hymns, "Heaven Came Down and Glory Filled My Soul." Then Cordy stood next to Callie as she read a tribute to Courtney – a poem, written a few days after Courtney's passing. My brother sang "Amazing Grace" and a close friend spoke beautifully. When my father approached the podium, I prayed for God to give him more strength than ever before. And strength was exactly what he exhibited. Using Courtney's notes, he delivered an exquisite tribute to an extraordinary girl, just another example of grace personified. Finally, a beautiful recording of "Somewhere over the Rainbow" played. It was actually the rendition I wanted for my own funeral. But coming home from Florida, I looked at Cordy and said, "I guess Courtney will be using my song." So, I gave my daughter one final gift. As the artist sang about bluebirds and rainbows, my heart cried. But the song brought a lightness to the atmosphere that seemed appropriate for Courtney. The service ended all too soon, taking me ever closer to saying goodbye. Walking out of that church behind my daughter's casket was excruciating; something no parent should ever have to experience. Words fail to capture the feelings of loss, unfairness, and finality.

Making our way to the car and the funeral procession, we began to notice something amazing. Everything was at a standstill. The street outside the church was lined with people standing at attention. As we headed out of town towards home, the procession continued for miles. Cars were pulled over with people standing beside them. More balloons and white bows adorned almost every building and sign. It took 45 minutes to park the cars at the graveside. After a few more words and another short prayer, it was over. We hugged and talked with people for a long time. It didn't seem to matter that it was a hot summer afternoon. People wanted to convey their love, and we desperately needed it. When the crowd finally left, we moved family and extended family into the house for a meal provided by our church.

I remember thinking that we'd made it through the worst part. I was wrong. Although the pain lessens over time, the sorrow of losing a child does not go away. Still, my new favorite word quickly became "overwhelmed" because God has never failed to provide grace to match the grief. That first day, He provided exactly what we needed for each moment and for each emotion, and He's continued to provide through the years. Some days require extraordinary measures, while other days are not as desperate. He is never taken aback by my weakness or my need. It reminds me of how the Lord provided manna in the wilderness for the Children of Israel. He never gave them a week's worth of food but only what they needed for that day. His faithfulness is new every morning. And yes, grace continues to carry us along.

Chapter 4:
Spiritual Preparation

Nothing can truly prepare us for the worst trials and troubles of life. What I have come to understand, however, is the importance of how I view life's tragedies and especially how I respond to them. Looking back, areas of my thinking were woefully unprepared for this kind of life event. But the most surprising thing has been recognizing what spiritual preparation actually looks like. The effort we put into our faith in Christ is never wasted time. God uses every bit of it for our good. Building spiritual disciplines such as Scripture memorization and prayer journaling are invaluable preparation for life's unexpected twists and turns. These habits became my life preservers after tragedy struck our family. So, before going any further in my story, I'd like to take a look back at my approach to life prior to Courtney's death and how God used my spiritual habits to change my thinking.

Preparation, planning, and goal-setting are very much a part of who I am. So much so, that friends and family sometimes tease me about it. Working from a plan has just always been my approach to life. So as I entered adulthood, I knew exactly how I wanted my life to look, and I had a plan to get there. Until 2011, my plan seemed to be working. There are times, however, when preparation morphs into inflexibility – especially when circumstances change. And as we all know, life has a way of going off script. These script changes are usually more frustrating than they are devastating. When my plan went completely off the rails I learned that being spiritually prepared is not the same as being in control.

My biggest mistake was in trying to control what my life looked like, what I thought a God-blessed life looked like. The script was changed in an instant; no amount of organization or preparation gave me control over it. And to make matters worse, I was questioning my view of the One who was in control. This definitely wasn't in my plan, but how was it possible that it was in God's plan? It's hard to wrap your thoughts around God's sovereignty when your child has just been brutally murdered. The issue of God's sovereignty in relation to tragedy in the life of a believer seems to be one of the biggest hurdles in Christian living. It certainly has been for me. As I mentioned in a previous chapter, one of my biggest struggles was suddenly viewing God as cruel rather than loving. My faith and my understanding have grown in this area since Courtney's death.

I sought answers both in Scripture and from those who spent their lives studying God's Word. In a 2016 interview with the *Kansas City Star*, Reverend Billy Graham was asked, "If God is all-powerful, doesn't that make him responsible for everything that happens, even evil?" His answer reveals wisdom that comes from studying and preaching God's Word for over 70 years. He said, "Let me assure you that God is not responsible for the evil in the world, nor will he ever do anything evil or wrong. The Bible says, *'His works are perfect, and all his ways are just. A faithful God who does no wrong, upright and just is he'* (Deuteronomy 32:4). Nor does God ever tempt us to do evil or make us do anything wrong. Admittedly God hasn't told us everything we'd like to know about evil and why it exists, but one thing is clear: God is not the author of evil, nor does he give in to its allure. The Bible says, *'God cannot be tempted by evil'* (James 1:13). Ultimately evil comes from Satan, who is absolutely opposed to God and to everything good."[1]

The Dangers of Being Spiritually Unprepared

Courtney's death was evil in every sense of the word. This kind of evil will exist as long as Satan roams the earth, which sets up an inevitable collision between good and evil. So yes, even faithful followers of Jesus experience the effects of evil. Because we cannot escape it, we often try to understand it. We struggle to make sense of senseless violence or to assign meaning to so called, "acts of God." In my opinion, this is where we fail in our preparedness to face life's worst tragedies. If we don't have a clear understanding of who God is and how He works, then tragedy can result in a crisis of faith. I can tell you from personal experience that a crisis of faith makes any other crisis even more devastating. For me, this came in the form of doubting God's love – something I had never felt before. In a nutshell, I trusted God with my soul – just not with earthly matters anymore. For a long time, I described this period of my life as my failure of faith. Although my faith was weak and misguided, it never truly failed. Once again, Scripture guided me to a deeper understanding, even of my own faith.

Believers often use the words *faith* and *salvation* synonymously. While they are deeply connected, notable aspects of each word affect our daily lives. John 3 describes salvation as being born again. We can get so accustomed to this word picture that we miss its implications. Once we are born, we cannot be unborn. Nor are we more born one day than another. Likewise, being born again is a fixed moment in the life of each believer. I think of it as being welded in place...immovable. Salvation is a covenant relationship sealed by the continual presence of the Holy Spirit (2 Corinthians 1:21-22).

John 10:28-29 reminds us that once we're saved, no one can pluck us out of His hand. So, I never doubted my position in God's family. This security was the bedrock of my spiritual preparation for tragedy. It gave me the freedom to be totally honest with God about my thoughts and my feelings. Even in my darkest moments, I knew the Holy Spirit was continually there, ministering to my broken heart.

Of course, salvation requires faith (Ephesians 2:8). This is where the words *faith* and *salvation* are used interchangeably. In general, faith describes having complete trust, belief, and confidence in something or someone. Salvation occurs the moment we place that trust in Jesus Christ. That's why we say a new Christian has "come to faith in Jesus." However, the faith we have at salvation is only a beginning point. The more we learn about God and His ways, the more we learn to trust Him, even when situations and circumstances change. As we exercise our faith, it grows (2 Thessalonians 1:3) and continual growth results in spiritual maturity.

The Bible uses different words to describe how we exhibit our faith at any given moment. The apostle Paul addresses believers whose faith is weak (Romans 14:1). And several times Jesus spoke of His followers having *"little faith"* (Matthew 6:30, 8:26, 14:31, and 16:8). It's interesting that these verses also contain phrases such as, *"Why are ye fearful"* and *"wherefore didst thou doubt?"* A crisis of faith results when: 1) we become disillusioned with the person in whom we have placed our faith; or 2) we're faced with having to place even greater trust in that person. My crisis was a combination of both things. When tragedy turned my life upside down, my untested faith proved to be weak, causing me to become disillusioned. I began to doubt that God had my best interest at heart, which resulted in hesitancy to trust Him at all, much less more.

The idea of a failure of faith occurs one place in Scripture, Luke 22:31-32. After the Last Supper, Jesus tells Peter, *"Simon, Simon, behold, Satan hath desired to have you, that he may sift you as wheat. But I have prayed for thee, that thy faith fail not: and when thou art converted, strengthen thy brethren."* In his book, *The Hard Sayings of Jesus,* author F.F. Bruce offers the following insights on this passage. "If those who had begun to follow [Jesus] were afraid that, under stress, they might deny him, they were assured that the Spirit's aid was available. If, however, they resisted the Spirit and rejected his aid, then indeed their case would be desperate. Peter, through fear, denied the Son of man, but he found forgiveness and restoration: his lips had momentarily turned traitor but his heart did not apostatize. His repentance left him wide open to the Spirit's healing grace, and when he was restored, he was able to strengthen others."[2]

I can sympathize with Peter. That's probably why he's one of my favorite people in the Bible. In my opinion, Peter is the original comeback kid. Although he is well-known for being impetuous and outspoken, Peter is also remembered for denying that he knew the Lord after Jesus was arrested. When Jesus predicted his denial just hours before, Peter vehemently argued that it would never – and could never – happen. Of course, we know that it did happen. Then after Jesus' death and resurrection, Peter was fully restored in his fellowship with the Lord. He went on to be an effective witness and preacher of the Gospel.

My favorite biblical example involving Peter is his experience walking on water. The full story is found in Matthew 14:22-34. Here's my abridged version. After the miracle of feeding the multitude, Jesus sent His disciples ahead of Him to the other side of the sea. When a huge storm came up suddenly, Jesus came to them by walking on the water. At first Peter was afraid. He wasn't sure it was actually Jesus. So, he asked for an invitation to go to the Lord on the water, knowing that if it was truly Jesus then all would be well. And it was. Peter walked on the water until he focused on the storm instead of on Jesus. As fear sank in, Peter began to sink. So, he called out to the Lord for help. Jesus caught him, pointed out his lack of faith, and led him back to the boat.

I'm struck by the fact that Jesus sent His disciples to the other side, knowing a storm was on the horizon. Since Peter was an avid fisherman, he had, no doubt, experienced storms at sea before – but probably never from outside the boat! Trusting Jesus in the midst of the stormy sea was a faith-stretching experience. It was preparation. And yet, after three years of sharing meals and conversations with the Lord, Peter had a crisis of faith. His lips spoke words that he could not have imagined just hours before.

Peter and I have much in common. After years of walking with Christ, I too thought my faith was strong. If God had told me on June 13, 2011, that I would completely doubt His love before the week ended, I would have said, "That could never happen!" However, I misjudged the depth and strength of my faith because it had not been tested in the storm. The storms of life look different from the shore than from the boat. And they definitely feel more intense when you're completely overboard, sinking in the billowing sea. Like Peter, my faith aspires to walk to the Lord atop my waves. But when my focus strays to life's troubles, my faith grows weak and I begin to sink. As long as my spiritual eyes are fixed on Jesus, my heart stays encouraged and our fellowship is close.

I can't help but believe that other followers of Jesus are going through the same kind of doubt that I experienced. If you feel ill-prepared to handle the circumstances you're currently facing, then I challenge you to address the following questions. First, do you have a genuine relationship with Jesus Christ, or do you just practice religion? Feeling as if you could turn away from God completely may mean that Jesus is not the object of your faith. You might have your faith in the wrong source. Salvation through Jesus Christ is the only firm foundation in this life. Second, how would you describe the current condition of your faith? Be completely honest with yourself. It's possible to be a Christian and have weak, small, or immature faith. If that's you, then be encouraged. Although I would never choose the path I'm now on, I've learned to know my Lord's heart in an even deeper way because of my experience. I have matured in my faith and in my understanding of the God I serve.

Godly Preparation

What I didn't realize prior to the summer of 2011 is that God's preparation often looks different than ours. I had mistakenly believed that faithfulness to God meant He would shield me from such heartache. In reality, He knew the tragedy I would face and was preparing me in ways I didn't see. Even as I write those words, I want to reiterate that no one can truly be prepared for this kind of devastation. I still went through a severe crisis of faith. It's only now that I see how faithful obedience gave me all of the tools I needed to strengthen my faith.

1) Knowledge of God's Word.

First, I had a good working knowledge of the Bible. This was largely due to coming to know the Lord at an early age and being raised in church. The Bible was central to my upbringing, as was an emphasis on memorizing Scripture. I cannot overstate the benefit of memorizing Scripture as preparation for life's storms. When Courtney died, I learned the truth of verses such as Psalm 4:1, *"God is our refuge* and strength, a very present help in trouble." And Psalm 119:11, *"Thy word have I hid in mine heart, that I might not sin against thee."* It's hard to imagine what my initial response would have been if so much of God's Word hadn't been in my heart and mind. I'll freely admit to not wanting to open my Bible at times. Even then, the Lord brought verses to the forefront of my mind that ministered to me in a way that nothing else could. Even verses I had forgotten I knew were there when I needed them. A verse that's been particularly meaningful is Joshua 1:8, *"This book of the law shall not depart out of thy mouth; but thou shalt meditate therein day and night, that thou mayest observe to do according to all that is written therein: for then thou shalt make thy way prosperous, and then thou shalt have good success."*

2) Growing up in a Christian home.

Another thing that played a huge role in my preparation was the example set by my parents. You might be thinking, "Of course, you're a preacher's daughter!" That definitely factors in. But in many ways, they were simply faithful followers of Christ who modeled consistency – as any Christian parent can do. Because they were generally transparent with us, I was able to observe how their faith worked when challenges and frustrations arose. Even when struggling with hurts from within the church walls, my parents didn't allow attacks of the enemy to distract or sideline them. Instead, they continued to grow spiritually. As a young girl, I wondered many times why they continued to put themselves through the frustration. But God's calling on their lives was definitive and non-negotiable. In reflection, I cannot explain how I observed their steadfast faith in adversity, yet missed that I too might face some kind of hardship. It somehow just didn't translate in my mind.

If you grew up with godly parents or grandparents, then you probably understand how easy it is to take them for granted. Their rules seem strict and their expectations often seem too high. One thing I know for certain – everything they did was motivated by unconditional love. Every expectation modeled the expectations of our heavenly Father. How else can you explain verses such as 1 Peter 1:16, *"Be ye holy, for I am holy."* They were building godly character into my life. Their continual influence was key to my spiritual backbone. And again, even then, I almost sank under the weight of despair. Being prepared spiritually doesn't mean you'll skate through life's toughest battles. If you're not fortified from within, then you're an easy target for the enemy. That's why 1 Peter 5:8 warns, *"Be sober, be vigilant; because your adversary the devil, as a roaring lion, walketh about, seeking whom he may devour."* We'll talk more about spiritual warfare in a later chapter.

As Christian parents, there's a tendency to hide our character flaws and cover up our past failures. Often, we try to shield our kids from the realities of evil and trouble in the world. I've come to believe that this can be a disservice to the next generation. Like my parents, I want to give my children the tools needed to live in a world ruled by their enemy. This requires authenticity and transparency. Yes, I need to model faithfulness to the Lord, but that doesn't mean projecting an image of spiritual perfection. Kids often learn more from our real struggles than from our façade of strength. How will they learn to acquire spiritual strength if I continually hide my struggles? I have been afforded many opportunities to display these traits to my children, both before and since our tragedy. My prayer is that Callie and Cole will continue to learn and grow as they watch me lean on the Lord with every fiber of my being.

Thinking back on how much my father influenced my life in similar ways, I find myself wiping back tears. Even though Daddy has gone on to be with the Lord, his spiritual legacy lives on. He taught me so much about loving and trusting God. I'm sure that he and my sweet daughter are catching up with each other in Heaven. God gave Daddy extended grace to preach Courtney's funeral. However, in the days, months, and years that followed, I watched him struggle with his own trust issues. While he knew the same principles I knew (and was the very one who taught them to me), his faith was also rocked. As difficult as those initial days were for me, I can't imagine how hard it was for him as a father, grandfather, and pastor. He was mourning the loss of his granddaughter, watching his daughter suffer inconsolably, and struggling to give our family what we needed spiritually. I've come to truly appreciate his transparency during those days. Even spiritual giants have to get through personal tragedy day by day, moment by moment. Because of Daddy's own wrestling with God, I didn't really have a pastor to go to with my questions and my anger. That would only have made his burden heavier. As a result, I had to learn reliance on my heavenly Father exclusively. Looking back, I believe this was as it should be.

3) Journaling my devotion time.

About two years prior to our heartbreak, I began to journal on a weekly basis. It was alternately a prayer journal and a diary of sorts. These weekly entries went hand-in-hand with my personal devotion time, which had lacked consistency into my early adulthood. As a young woman, I genuinely wanted to serve God with all of my heart, but it took some failure before finally getting a handle on how important a daily time with God truly is. I heard that it takes thirty days to form a habit, whether good or bad. So, I wrote myself reminder notes and stuck with it until my quiet time was a natural part of my day. What I once viewed as a chore became something I looked forward to. Adding weekly journaling to my devotion was the same way.

I found that it helped to get my thoughts, and even my anxieties, down on paper. Both before and after my tragedy, I went back and read my prayers, remembering how God had answered various requests and helped me navigate difficult situations. As encouraging as this was, I often became disappointed with myself because reading those entries revealed how much energy I spent worrying in vain. My frustration would intensify later, as my family walked through our darkest days. In my grief and frustration, many lessons that I thought had been firmly set had actually been forgotten and would need to be learned all over again. Over time, journaling has guided me to the truth and power behind 1 Peter 5:7, *"Casting all your care upon him; for He careth for you."*

It's interesting to read back through my journal entries from before Courtney's death. That's where I first realized God had been preparing me for the battle. We are such forgetful creatures. I feel a similarity to the Children of Israel, who continually forgot how God had provided for them in the past. He constantly reminded them of His deep kindness, love, and care. Thankfully, God's patience with us is never exhausted. He is not nearly as hard on me as I sometimes am on myself. Without my knowing it, God was using my journal to prepare me for the storm to come.

After our tragedy, healing took place each time I journaled. It was an outlet for my grief. Many of my emotions were like roadblocks to trusting the Lord again. Because my journal was strictly between God and me, I wrote down thoughts I couldn't verbalize to another living soul. Some of them were not pretty. In fact, many of them were downright ugly. But since those thoughts were real, He already knew them. As the anger and despair poured from my heart to the paper, the ugly thoughts were replaced with cries for help. Little by little, those cries for help became glimmers of hope. And eventually, those glimmers of hope became thankfulness. Yes, I became thankful for what God was teaching me and was able to recognize His hand at work in my life. What a beautiful gift this became for my hurting heart.

My preparedness has been tested by fire. Still, I thank God that He knew what I would face. I've had to relinquish control. I've learned to trust Him, not only with the tragedy in my past, but with every "what if" of my future. My faith, though beaten and battered, has emerged stronger than ever before. Not because He's shielded me from life's storms, but because He holds my hand as we walk together on top of the waves. Nothing is sadder than hearing of professing Christians who have turned their backs on God because He allowed adversity into their lives. No matter how weak or strong you think your faith is, please don't refuse help from the only One who makes it possible to survive after the waves have receded. The only way to truly prepare for life's tragedies is to be in close fellowship with our Creator and Sustainer. A phrase that often runs across my mind is, "When you can't trace God's hand, trust His heart." To me, that sums up what faith in Jesus Christ really means.

Chapter 5:
We're Not a Statistic

As I woke up the morning after Courtney's funeral, I was numb. The mad rush of the past week was over. Out of town family returned home, and our friends returned to work. They had made sure we had plenty of food and that our house and yard were in order. The four of us didn't have to be at work or school. We were just there…in a quiet house. So, I walked out onto my porch with my Bible, trying to find some peace in the midst of the quiet. Cordy came out to join me after I read for quite a while. Although we both felt at a loss for words, we reflected on the past week. Had it really been only a week since our world stopped turning? Yes, exactly one week before we had fallen to our knees in those first moments and begged God to help us. And He most certainly had done that time and time again in the last seven days. But we could not wrap our hearts or minds around what to do next. The more we talked the more one thing became clear – we had a decision to make. We could either crawl into the hole left by Courtney's loss, or we could keep trusting God and keep moving. While neither choice brought our baby back, the dangers of not being proactive were just too great.

The Statistical Danger Zone

In the years since Courtney's death, we've become painfully aware of the statistical data and psychology behind tragedies like ours. Two main concerns crossed my mind. First, the loss of a child tends to magnify the weaknesses in a relationship. Many marriages don't survive. The hardest struggles come in the quiet days and months after the initial event, a lesson we were about to learn firsthand. Even strong Christian marriages are not indestructible when intense grief enters the equation. Prior to our loss, we knew families that had lost children; their marriages weakened to the point of complete failure. The divorce rate is especially high in situations where blame can potentially be placed. Psychologists say the tendency to blame is particularly strong when a child is killed while in the care of one parent.[3] Although Cordy had been there, I'm the one who verbally gave Courtney permission to walk down the beach that day. How would that decision affect our marriage in the days ahead?

My other concern was for Callie and Cole. I've learned volumes about grief, through both personal experience and lots of reading. And everything I've read about siblings and grief validates my concerns. The kids would have to face many issues that Cordy and I would not. Typically, parents receive most of the care and attention when a child dies. As the surviving children watch their parents deal with such devastating loss, many are hesitant to express their own feelings of grief. Maybe that's why sibling grief is often misunderstood. If left alone, many kids struggle with confusing thoughts and emotions, or they push their feelings aside altogether. It's not unusual for grieving siblings to deal with anxiety, abandonment, and survivor's guilt. I've heard it said like this: "When a parent dies, you lose the past.[4] When a child dies, you lose the future. When a sibling dies you lose the past and the future." How would Callie and Cole cope with all this? And how could Cordy and I help them when we barely knew how to help ourselves?

The Only Way Out is Through

That morning on the porch, Cordy and I decided that our family would not become one of those statistics. For our sakes and for Courtney's sake, we had to start living again. That concept sounded impossible. At the time I couldn't have voiced our exact plan. My mind was still too muddled for that kind of clear thinking. It's best summed up in a phrase I saw recently, "The only way out is through." God showed me this principle in numerous ways over the next few years. At times, my grief felt like an enormous dark forest; and I was lost in the midst of it. There was no way to be air lifted out or magically transported to a more peaceful place. The only way out of grief's darkest places is to walk right through it. But it's hard to make out the path clearly in that kind of enveloping darkness. Some people wander in this darkness for years after a devastating loss. When a child is taken suddenly at a young age, it's easy to curl up on the forest floor and just stop walking altogether. This was exactly what Cordy and I were determined not to do. If our world was going to start turning again, then we had to keep moving. So, we just took one step at a time, trusting God to shine the light and lead the way.

Expressing Gratitude

Taking the next step was often a matter of just doing the next thing. So, I began to write thank you notes for all of the flowers, food, and gifts. I cannot tell you how helpful this was. Each card filled my heart with gratitude for the family and friends surrounding us. These notes became much more than just an exercise in proper etiquette. Expressing genuine gratitude focused my mind in the right direction – God's direction. Every heartfelt gesture that had been poured out on us was a tangible expression of God's love and concern for our family. And in the difficult days ahead, He kept reminding us of His love through the care of other people. For instance, friends periodically dropped by with food or left small gifts at our back door. Sometimes it was little things like seeing white bows remain on mailboxes and houses long after the funeral. And cards continued to come in the mail for months, and even years.

People often wonder if a small gesture actually helps in the face of devastating tragedy. Yes, it does! These demonstrations of love and care became a regular part of our conversations at night. As we shared about our day, we started to verbally express gratitude again. We talked about all the ways God was giving us a daily measure of His grace – individually and as a family. I truly believe that these conversations were a big part of why we survived. They brought us together in a new kind of bond that only the four of us could share. Even today, I'm humbled and amazed.

Walking the Path Together

It may sound naïve that Cordy and I simply decided to not become a statistic. After all, we're not the first couple to face this kind of tragedy; no couple plans to purposely fail or throw in the towel. So, why have we survived? How has our marriage grown even stronger in the years since Courtney was taken from us? Put simply, we left our porch that morning committed to walking through this dark forest together. Of course, multiple factors come into play in any family tragedy. As I've read what psychologists say determines a couple's survival, I recognized several things that helped us stay on the path, hand-in-hand.[5]

First, the stronger a relationship is prior to a loss the better its chance of survival. This simple concept was probably the most important for us. As Christians, we've always held to the belief that a strong relationship includes a foundation built on Christ. This was true even before we knew each another. Cordy accepted Jesus as his Savior early in life, just as I had done. So, when we met (after graduating college), we were both looking for a spouse who was a strong believer. We felt that we had each waited for the other to come along. Our decision to marry after just nine months of dating was largely due to knowing exactly what we each wanted in a spouse. We desired a home centered around Jesus Christ and were determined that this marriage was forever. I can honestly say that Cordy is my best friend, in every sense of the word.

Another important factor in our survival is how much support we received after losing Courtney. The care shown to us that first week was overwhelming because it came from every direction. Our strongest supporters, however, were simply doing what they had always done for us. Our extended families have a closer than average bond. We've become one big family unit over time. In addition to loving each other, we all share a love for God. Having children further sealed the bond we shared. Courtney was the first grandbaby on both sides of our family; so her birth had been highly anticipated. From the beginning, we had more help and support than we needed at times. And that didn't change when Callie and Cole came along. Through the years, both sets of grandparents have been a great source of help – both physically and spiritually. The support we received on a regular basis naturally extended to this – our greatest challenge. Our families continue to be there for us and to love our children beyond words.

That circle of strong support extends to our community. We love living in Toombs County, Georgia. Both of us came to this small town with our parents by the time we were young adults. This is where we met and married. And because it's a great environment in which to raise children, it's where we choose to make our home. Early in our marriage, the close-knit atmosphere that enveloped us was out of our comfort zone at times. However, there are so many benefits to living in a place where everyone is your neighbor. Many of our closest friendships were built through mutual activities and events involving the kids. These friendships evolved to a point that we felt we had known them forever.

When we lost Courtney so tragically, our friends and our town were devastated with us. They showed up in droves to let us know how much we were loved. And their expressions of love extended far beyond food and flowers. For instance, Courtney's soccer team dedicated the first game of the season in her honor. Many people from the community came out that night to pay their respects. The soccer coach retired Courtney's jersey and number; then they released balloons as a tribute. Later, our church youth group secretly finished Courtney's FFA project – restoring an old Ford 8N tractor. Our community was there again, donating every dollar needed and even arranging a surprise dedication ceremony. Also, several scholarships were created in Courtney's name. One of them has enough money to renew for at least 20 years. That's why writing thank you notes didn't stop after the funeral. That exercise served as a reminder of our community's love and support. Each act of extreme kindness helped draw our family together. Even through the tears, I knew that we were blessed beyond measure.

The factor presenting our greatest challenge was how we lost Courtney. My concern was that one of us would eventually blame the other for Courtney's death; for not recognizing something amiss in that boy's character. And in situations like ours, the research and statistics were certainly stacked against us. In our case, however, the blame game never happened. I believe the answer to why our marriage avoided this particular pothole comes down to one word

– communication. We acknowledged early on that our marriage would have to be strong to survive this. As we began to talk more openly about our individual feelings of guilt, we realized that neither of us blamed the other. Somehow, we both felt personally responsible for what happened without extending those feelings to each other. So, even though we both dealt with self-judgment daily, we came together as a couple and talked about it. We shared ways that God was helping us heal. Remarkably, this was a sweet time for our marriage. It was a kind of vulnerability we had not experienced prior to our loss; it strengthened our bond rather than weakened it. What a blessing of God's grace!

Grieving Differently

Looking back, I see that each of us grieved for Courtney differently; and that was okay. Keeping lines of communication open was important for the entire family. That meant allowing emotions to be expressed and not trying to fit one another's grief into our personal mold. Before Cordy and I could help the kids, we had to learn how to do this.

Our grief seemed to match our personalities. While I'm outgoing and talkative, Cordy is more the strong, silent type. So, his way of coping was to not dwell on it by staying busy. In hindsight, this is how he handled the sorrow, even from those first moments in Florida. Immediately after receiving the news, he began packing up her belongings. I'm not sure if he sat down much over those initial days. He cried when he stopped, so he just never stopped. This way may or may not have helped; it was just his way. Because I expressed my grief more openly and more often, Cordy tried to keep me distracted, too. He would tell me to change the channel in my mind when a wave of grief hit. Our differences became a struggle.

One night stands out. We walked to Courtney's resting place, lit a small candle in the lantern, and sat on the swing to talk and decompress. This was something we did a lot in the early period of our grief. It was comforting. On this particular night, however, I was overcome. Cordy, not knowing what to say because he was struggling with his own grief, reminded me to think about other things. This was more than I could bear. So, with tears streaming down my face, I begged him to let me grieve in my own way. Of course, I know he was only trying to comfort and protect me; it was pure love. But attempting to cope with my grief in his way was just too much for me.

Fortunately, Cordy didn't take offense. As he gave me the opportunity to express my feelings and share my fears, I found the words I needed. I had tried to be strong for everyone, including him; and I couldn't do it anymore. After I opened up, Cordy talked about his own anger and confusion. We took turns, allowing thoughts, questions, and emotions to flow freely. Although neither of us could take away the other person's grief, we agreed that understanding each other's grief was crucial. Just as Cordy could not force me to ignore the pain, I could not force him to express his pain the way I did. So, if he did not want to say a lot most days…that was all right. Sitting there in the glow of the lantern, we realized that this was going to be a long battle. And honestly, we were scared of the toll all this could take on our relationship. That conversation helped immensely. It opened the door for both of us to say things we had previously been afraid to say. This open dialogue continued in the days ahead. We used our time alone at Courtney's place to talk about the details and frustrations the kids didn't need to know. Despite the fact that our whole world was upside down, we didn't doubt our love for each other.

Of course, the kids grieved differently as well. Callie faced a myriad of emotions when Courtney died. I believe she experienced extreme survivor's guilt because she could easily have been the one asked to take a walk that day. She felt robbed of not just her best friend, but her partner in life. You see, the girls were only seventeen months apart in age and looked a lot alike. While they had opposite temperaments and interests, their differences didn't limit their friendship. They confided in each other about every area of their lives. Initially Callie shut down and didn't say much of anything. Then her feelings found words in the beautiful poem she wrote for Courtney's funeral. As time went on, she began to grieve more openly, but she still put on a brave face.

Callie also went from being the middle child to being the oldest. Now, she would be the first to reach goals and milestones. Rather than considering this a privilege, it was almost like an unwanted responsibility. God helped her with this difficult adjustment over time. Callie had accepted Christ several years before and was growing as a Christian. She spent time writing out Scripture that encouraged her and being involved with the Fellowship of Christian Athletes. Even though the sudden loss of her sister was a big challenge to face, Callie is a strong and resilient girl. As time progressed, the qualities instilled in her have risen to the surface. She is a shining light of grace and hope for those around her.

Cole's immediate reaction to Courtney's death was intense. After the first few days, however, he didn't say much and grew quieter by the day. I guess he handled grief the only way he knew how... silence. Cole was only 11 years old and had accepted Christ about a year before. It was such a tender time in his young Christian life. I worried that this experience could cause him to turn from God completely. Cole and Courtney had been very close. Even when Courtney appeared to be irritated by Cole following her around the farm, we all knew how much she cared for him. She was his protector and counselor. As time went on, Cole found his own way of coping. He would go off for long periods of time just to be alone in a place on the farm he and Courtney had once enjoyed together. He felt her loss deeply. We just didn't force him to talk about his grief. Just as Cordy and I had done with each other, we simply kept communication lines open so that he felt free to grieve in his own way. Of course, we also reminded him every day that we were there when he was ready to talk.

One day, about six months after Courtney's death, Cole called and asked me to come get him from school. He sounded upset but was doing all he could to keep from crying. After checking him out at the office, we sat quietly in my car in the school parking lot. I asked, "What's up buddy?" He told me he needed some assurance in his relationship with God and just needed to be with me for a few minutes. We talked about how much God loved him, then we prayed together. He seemed to calm down and finally told me he was ready to go back to class. It was a simple moment, yet it was one of the sweetest moments I've experienced as a mother. Over the years, Cole has continued to deal with our loss in his own way and in his own time. I have watched God grow my little boy into a fine young man with a strong mind and a caring heart. He loves the Lord and is growing in his Christian walk every day.

As Normal as Possible

Cordy and I reached several conclusions during that conversation on our porch the day after Courtney's funeral. The bottom line was that our family had to start living again. The longer we waited, the harder it would be. Now that the funeral was behind us, Cordy and I had to continue with our daily responsibilities. Our new day-to-day life proved to be more challenging than we imagined. Still, we were determined to survive. (More about that in the next chapter.) Our biggest concern was for our kids. This tragedy would undoubtedly impact their lives. And while we couldn't change that, we didn't want them to live in its dark shadow forever. My heart's desire was to help them find their own identity and not just be Courtney's little brother and sister. So, we tried to make their lives as normal as possible; and that meant returning to daily routines.

All of us benefited from being active again, but Callie seemed to gain the most from it. A few months before Courtney died, Callie bravely decided to try out for cheerleading. She had never cheered before but thought she would like it. At first, she struggled with learning the choreography for the try-outs, as well as adhering to the strict dress code. She kept at it and successfully made the team. Even though Courtney hadn't been interested in cheering herself, she was very proud of Callie and applauded her courage and perseverance. Courtney's approval meant so much to her. Then on the trip home from Florida, Callie said she didn't want to continue cheerleading. And while I totally understood her feelings, I asked her to give it a few weeks before making that decision. She finally chose to continue, thinking it might even be fun. I'm so thankful for the little things. Callie's cheerleading proved to be a balm for her aching heart. Her "cheer sisters" took her under their wings and kept her smiling and laughing through some tough days. She was able to be more than just Courtney's little sister. She was able to feel like a normal high-school girl, if even for a little while.

As time went on, we each began to find our way to some kind of new normal, not just individually but as a whole. We had made our decision. Since the only way out of this dark forest was through, then we would continue to walk hand-in-hand…refusing to become another statistic. Yes, we had weathered the storm of the last week. I just didn't consider what the aftermath would be.

Chapter 6:
The Aftermath of the Storm

Just as every storm has an aftermath, every tragedy has after effects. The way we emerged from continual crisis mode was similar to those surveying the damage of a huge storm. It was impossible to see all the destruction at once. As a matter of fact, it would be many months before we knew the extent of the harm. The aftermath would prove to be almost as devastating as the storm itself.

Days turned into weeks and weeks turned into months. The kids were back in school, Cordy was back at work, and I returned to my catering business. Although I had a few jobs lined up, my heart wasn't really in it. Still, staying busy was better because the quiet was terrifying. So, to keep from total despair I tried to fill up every moment of the day. During this time, I accepted a part-time job with the Fellowship of Christian Athletes, which was a blessing. Not only did it give me something to do, it also offered an opportunity to impact kids. We continued serving in our church, as well as spending daily time in prayer and Bible study. We rocked along in this pattern for a few months. The sun kept coming up every day and going down every night. I was existing and almost peaceful at times. Then another wave of grief would hit.

The investigators and prosecutors in Florida sent periodic updates about evidence, witnesses, forensics, and a myriad of other details. We really didn't want to hear any of it, but we needed to be aware of how the case was unfolding. From the outset, they told us it could take close to two years for the trial to begin. Of course, that was frustrating, considering the perpetrator was in custody and it seemed to be a straightforward case. We hoped it would happen sooner, knowing that any healing we might experience would probably be undone during a murder trial. Like drowning victims, we grasped for whatever life preserver we could find.

As miserable as those days were, I see now how faith sustained us. I do not say this lightly; my emotions were raw and real. My thoughts were often not at all lined up with God's thoughts. Frankly, many of my deepest feelings were too embarrassing to share with anyone except the Lord. When I occasionally told my mother about these no-holds-barred conversations with God, she would say, "You can't talk to God like that." Perhaps she was right; but He already knew that my thoughts and words were coming from a place of hurt and confusion. He is a big God. He can handle anything we send His way. Because the Lord saw my heart completely, He also knew that my ultimate desire was to somehow use this horrific tragedy for good. Otherwise, it all seemed to be a waste. Even so, the depth of my pain stayed veiled by a mask of bravery.

My façade began to unravel after about six months. It was January and even in South Georgia everything outside looked cold and depressing. My spirit died along with the foliage. Around this time, I also became ill. It was really just a bad cold, but the symptoms were not merely physical. I didn't care about anything. I wanted to die. My only reason for getting out of bed most days was to maintain some kind of normalcy for my other two children. One night, on a visit to Courtney's resting place, I lay down beside her and began to cry inconsolably. I had only cried that way a handful of times. My sobbing was so intense that I made myself even more ill. Then, without any breeze at all, the wind chimes under Courtney's gazebo rang three times. It was surreal. To my mind, even though Courtney could no longer speak to me, it was her love for me that spoke in that moment. God used a simple wind chime to remind me that Courtney was all right now. This was an important shifting point mentally and emotionally. In spite of the proclamation, "I am fine," I was the furthest thing from fine. Instead of dealing with the aftermath of our storm, I had been wrestling to make sense of it. It was time to come out of my bunker and face the damage. I needed to clean up the debris scattered throughout my heart and mind.

Almost immediately after we lost Courtney, a dear friend offered professional Christian counseling, which I politely declined. Then on the night of my breakdown I called her. The only words I could manage were, "I'm ready to talk." It was as if the Holy Spirit had also told her it was time. She simply said, "Oh! Thank God." We began weekly sessions almost immediately. Taking off my mask of bravery wasn't easy. During those first sessions, I maintained that I just needed someone to talk with. But as I began to open up with her, delving into my innermost thoughts and feelings, we discovered this was going to be a long journey. My heart was more than broken; it was shattered.

Regular counseling uncovered the underlying fact of my condition – I was angry with God. My faith (the faith I touted to everyone I met) was not nearly as strong as I once believed. It had never truly been tested. My misconceptions about God were a weak foundation. So, Courtney's death came through like a tornado and left me in a heap of rubble. I desperately needed to strengthen my faith, which required believing that, *"The Lord is my rock, and my fortress, and my deliverer; my God, my strength, in whom I will trust; my buckler, and the horn of my salvation, and my high tower* (Psalm 18:2). As my counseling sessions became more honest, I began to put a name on what was happening in my heart – it was spiritual warfare. That's when it hit me. It was not grief alone that was rocking my faith. I was under attack and this was going to be the battle of my life.

My Personal Battle

When I was a little girl, we sang "I'm in the Lord's Army" in Sunday school. The truth behind this little song is more than we can possibly understand as children. 2 Timothy 2:3 says to *"endure hardness, as a good soldier of Jesus Christ."* So, as a Christian, I should always be prepared for battle. Military personnel understand the importance of preparation, even in peacetime. They endure extreme training so they won't be caught off guard by surprise attacks. They are able to fight effectively in the heat of battle as they draw from their training. Even if the battle does not come for many years, the wise soldier continues his or her training in order to be ready for the enemy. Similarly, I had been in training for spiritual warfare most of my life. Reading God's Word, being faithful to Christian service, and growing in Christ were preparation for the battles to come. Even then, I was certainly not looking for a fight. It took time to regroup and realize what was happening. Spiritual warfare looks different for each of us. My personal battlefield was the loss of my child. It was there I had to wage war against my own fear, doubt, and pride, not to mention battling the enemy's lies.

Recognizing My Enemy

Many wars start with a single shot fired. My war began on a bright, sunny day at the beach. Who was I fighting? Who wanted so desperately to destroy me? It's nearly impossible to win a war against an unknown enemy. In a military sense, no general goes into battle without first learning everything he can about the enemy's tactics. The same principle is true spiritually. We need to be aware of who our enemy is and how he operates. Only one person celebrated when my sweet daughter was taken from us – Satan. Several years later, my mother told me a story; and the visual has stayed with me. Our hometown experienced a bad storm on the day Courtney died. That night, as my family left town coming to us, they passed a house that had been struck by lightning. Looking at the house engulfed in fire, my father commented that it felt like the devil and all his demons were dancing in the flames. It pictured the devastation we all felt. A living nightmare. Ever since, that's how I've pictured the enemy's celebration.

Because Satan hates God, he is every Christian's arch enemy. Now, he wasn't always evil. He was a created being named Lucifer who served under God's authority. In his pride, however, Lucifer led a rebellion against his Creator and was cast from Heaven, along with those who joined him. This same attitude of rebellion introduced sin into the world. Since that time, the devil and his demonic army have wreaked havoc on mankind. Even though Jesus' resurrection defeated Satan, that victory won't be fully experienced until Christ returns. Until then, the devil rules all the wickedness in the world. Knowing full well that the war is lost, he attempts to take as many as possible with him into eternal punishment. Of course, he cannot alter the eternal destiny of God's children, so he looks for ways to hurt and discourage followers of Jesus Christ. He will do anything (and I mean anything) to hinder our spiritual growth and destroy our influence in the world. Why God allows this leeway is still an enigma to me.

The enemy also knows exactly which blows are most capable of crippling us spiritually. We're most vulnerable to his attacks when we are weak or wounded. Weeping next to Courtney's grave was my weakest moment yet, and the enemy knew I was vulnerable. By whispering lies, he had stirred up so much fear and doubt that I was almost paralyzed spiritually. In my sadness and confusion, I had forgotten to stay alert. God also knew I was vulnerable in that moment, and He was waiting for me to reach out to Him...to trust Him again.

Of all the things I've learned about spiritual warfare, a few stand out. First, I dislike the devil as much as he dislikes me. After all, he is the author of evil. He is the reason that sin exists in the world. So, I could stop trying to make sense of this tragedy. Satan is ultimately the reason my sweet daughter lost her life, and he is not the least bit contrite. Secondly, I do not want Satan to achieve even the tiniest victory in my life. This determination became my new motivation. If I don't want him to be victorious over me, then I won't let him be. And yes, that's more easily said than done. I had forgotten that it was not up to me to win these battles. I simply needed to admit I was weak and to call out to my Defender. Finally, as followers of Jesus Christ, we have all the tools needed to resist the enemy, we sometimes just fail to utilize them. I had forgotten to put on my spiritual armor. Praise be to God...this was not the end of my story.

Putting My Armor Back On

Spiritual armor prepares us for the enemy's attacks as we make every effort to live for Christ. Ephesians 6:11 instructs believers to

"Put on the whole armor of God." I was introduced to this passage as a child. In my mind's eye, I can see the poster that hung in my Sunday school room. A soldier, in full regalia, stood ready for battle. Yet, my young mind couldn't fully grasp the meaning of this passage. *"For we wrestle not against flesh and blood, but against principalities, against powers, against the rulers of the darkness of this world, against spiritual wickedness in high places"* (Ephesians 6:12). Now I was on the front lines. I had experienced what the full forces of evil could do, and I knew I was in danger of further attacks.

Ephesians 6 describes five pieces of defensive armor we are to keep with us daily, as well as our only offensive weapon – *"the sword of the Spirit, which is the Word of God"* (v17). Scripture is the only thing that sustained me during those early months. As I said in chapter one, God's Word is what corrected my misconceived notions. Still, there were days that the pain of my loss was the only emotion that won my time and attention. It was often sheer determination to survive that drove me to God's Word. The verses I had learned over the years came flooding back in my mind. Even verses that were a little fuzzy helped because I remembered enough to find them in my Bible. Knowing how to wield my sword was not my problem. I had been properly trained. Simply put, I was susceptible to injury because I had momentarily laid down some of my defensive armor. As I began to purposely put each piece back in its place, victory seemed possible again.

Battling Lies

Satan is a liar and has perfectly honed his craft. Anything that comes from him is twisted in order to discourage and deceive. God, on the other hand, deals in truth; and truth is powerful. The only way to battle the lies of the enemy is with the belt of truth. *"Stand therefore, having your loins girt about with truth…"* (Ephesians 6:14). Satan had effectively bombarded my mind with lies because I had briefly taken off my belt. He repeatedly whispered that I had brought this on myself by allowing Courtney to walk down that beach. He said that I would never experience joy in my life again. He told me I would never survive this, and there was no point in trying anymore because I was already defeated. But the greatest lie was that God had broken His promises and was no longer trustworthy.

There were at least four or five moments during this period that I pictured myself lying down on the battlefield and waving a white flag. Of course, I didn't actually want to surrender to the enemy; I just didn't want to fight anymore. In my weakened faith, he convinced me that defeat was inevitable. I felt that I would never be effective for Christ again. That's the thing about emotions – they're deceptive. God, however, continued to present me with the truth as I read my Bible daily.

So, I hung the sword of the Spirit on my belt of truth – where it belonged! I began to speak truth out loud, quoting the verses God put in front of me. When I spoke God's Word, the enemy had no choice other than to flee, taking his lies with him. Even on the days my heart struggled to believe, speaking truth out loud was a reminder of my victory in Christ. Now, I can confidently say, *"Who shall separate us from the love of Christ? Shall tribulation, or distress, or persecution, or famine, or nakedness, or peril, or sword? As it is written, for thy sake we are killed all the day long; we are accounted as sheep for the slaughter. Nay, in all these things we are more than conquerors through him that loved us. For I am persuaded, that neither death, nor life, nor angels, nor principalities, nor powers, nor things present, nor things to come, nor height, nor depth, nor any other creature, shall be able to separate us from the love of God, which is in Christ Jesus our Lord"* (Romans 8:35-39).

Battling Fear

Fear presents itself in many ways: worry, anxiety, fretfulness, etc. One thing is certain…we've all experienced fear in one form or another. While moments of being afraid may come and go, our minds should be ruled by the peace of God, not by our fears. Ephesians 6 presents peace as the shoes in our spiritual armor. Verse 15 says, *"And your feet shod with the preparation of the gospel of peace."* The Gospel of Jesus Christ offers peace with God (Romans 5:1). Through saving faith, we enter God's family and are no longer His enemies. The gospel of peace is what enables us to stand our ground in spiritual battles. Put another way, peace *with* God gives us the peace *of* God. Yet fear is often a very real battle for many believers. It certainly has been for me. In my weakest moments, experiencing the peace of God in my heart and mind was extremely difficult. Of course, the problem was that I had gone to battle barefoot! I was not wearing my shoes of peace, as I had been trained to do.

We tend to know our greatest fears. You know, the things that occupy your mind in the dead of night. For many, it's being alone – either losing or never having a mate. For others, it might be financial loss or health worries. A very common fear is losing a beloved friend or family member. Those of us who have children often worry that something bad will happen to one of them. This was always my ultimate fear. I had no doubt our babies were precious gifts from God. So, like many parents, we dedicated our children to the Lord, giving them back to Him. Still, when I prayed over them each night, I asked God to make me a worthy mother. One of my misconceptions was that God expected me to be a perfect mother, that He would no longer trust me with these children if I failed in any way. If I'm totally honest, I thought I was praying a sort of insurance policy around them to secure their safety. Yet another misconception.

So, in the initial moments of not being able to find Courtney, this old fear became gut-wrenching despair. Even though I was hoping against hope for a good outcome, I experienced classic symptoms of fearing the worst: sweaty palms, nervous stomach, and continual pacing. While not knowing where she was felt unbearable, knowing was even worse. Once we learned the reality of our situation, other fears developed. How would this affect my other children? Would my marriage survive? Would I ever be happy again? All of these were legitimate fears that needed to be given over to God.

Several places in Scripture helped me to, once again, lace up my shoes of peace as I battled various fears. Psalm 23:4 speaks to the fear of death, *"Yea, though I walk through the valley of the shadow of death, I will fear no evil: for thou art with me; thy rod and thy staff they comfort me."* I remember a sermon on this particular verse that gave me great comfort. The word "through" is crucial. We do not stay in the *"valley of the shadow;"* we *"walk through"* it. Neither do we travel this dark valley alone. The Shepherd is with us, to guide and comfort. Reflecting on this verse, I realized that this promise illustrated exactly how God was helping me. Yes, I was walking through the valley of my worst fear, but God was walking with me and would not leave me there to grieve alone. Then came this glorious thought – He had not left Courtney either! After all, the worst thing the devil can throw at us is death, which is still no match for being ushered into God's heavenly presence.

Isaiah 41:10 reminds me that no situation is too great for Him. *"Fear thou not; for I am with thee: be not dismayed; for I am thy God: I will strengthen thee; yea, I will help thee; yea, I will uphold thee with the right hand of my righteousness."* Even before our tragedy, I knew my strength came from the Lord. Yet, nothing I'd experienced to this point in life had forced me to cling to Him so desperately. Being *dismayed* was unfamiliar territory, to say the least. I suddenly found myself weakened and wounded by my circumstances, which made me an easy target for the enemy. Even if I could have lived in my own strength, I had none left. All of my misconceptions had been stripped away. Any previous idea that I was tough was long gone. The key to surviving any form of tragedy or despair is Philippians 4:13: *"I can do all things through Christ which strengtheneth me."* Now, I strive to intentionally live each day in God's strength, trusting Him to uphold me with His righteous right hand.

Although our worst fears seldom come to pass, sometimes they do. My trust in God's faithfulness eroded in a moment. I've since learned that trust and peace go hand-in-hand. I love Isaiah 26:3, *"Thou wilt keep him in perfect peace, whose mind is stayed on thee: because he trusteth in thee."* I think we drive peace away by focusing on the "whys," "what ifs," and "if onlys" in life, rather than maintaining focus completely on Christ. My tragedy taught me what real peace means. It is not an absence of trouble; it's the absolute presence of God.

Battling Doubt

Because my belief system was fractured, everything I previously thought about how God works was in disarray. My mind could not connect the loving God I had always known to the God who allowed this tragedy to take place. Although I never verbalized that God was no longer trustworthy, I certainly thought it. Doubting God weakened my faith, which opened the door for the enemy to get a foothold. Ephesians 6:16 describes the piece of armor I needed, *"Above all, taking the shield of faith, wherewith ye shall be able to quench all the fiery darts of the wicked."* In his commentary on Ephesians, Warren Wiersbe says, "The 'faith' mentioned here is not saving faith, but rather living faith, a trust in the promises and the power of God."[6] So, while my faith was real and in the right person, it was not strong. I couldn't quench the darts of doubt because my shield was laid aside. The enemy took full advantage of this opening in my armor and planted seeds of doubt about God's love and care for my family.

My desire was to emerge from this tragedy with a testimony of God's grace and mercy, but my humanity was struggling with indescribable loss. This was my child, my heart, my hopes. During this time, I greatly identified with the father in Mark 9 who asked Jesus to heal his child. Verse 24 says, *"And straightway the father of the child cried out, and said with tears, Lord, I believe; help thou mine unbelief."* This was me! Although I still believed, my trust was wavering. I was like the double minded man in James 1:8, *"...unstable in all his ways."*

Then, I discovered something I'd never thought about before. Only God is all knowing. For years I believed the enemy could get into my head and know all my thoughts and fears. This is not the case. He cannot read our minds. In truth, the devil knew I was vulnerable because I told him I was. I told him exactly how to attack when I said, "Where is God when I need Him?" By speaking my insecurities and doubts out loud, I gave the enemy all the fiery darts he needed at the exact moment I was lowering my shield.

So, during this period of questioning, I learned to take my doubts to God in silent prayer. This is not to say I came to God with an ugly heart or impertinent thoughts. My respect for His holiness had not changed. Yet, I needed to give words to the brokenness and doubt plaguing me. I simply did not know how. Countless times, the Holy Spirit ministered to me in such an amazing way. Each time I asked Him to help me pray, He gave me the words to speak and breathed peace over my bruised heart. The promises of Romans 8:26-27 became evident, *"Likewise the Spirit also helpeth our infirmities: for we know not what we should pray for as we ought: but the Spirit itself maketh intercession for us with groanings which cannot be uttered.*

And he that searcheth the hearts knoweth what is the mind of the Spirit, because he maketh intercession for the saints according to the will of God." I do not believe the Father is disappointed when doubts arise, as long as we turn to Him rather than turn away. In my raw and wounded state, He covered me with His grace and mercy and began replacing those doubts with renewed faith.

Battling Pride

The majority of my spiritual battles after Courtney's death were head-on assaults. Satan's attacks with lies, fear, and doubt were neither subtle nor surprising. My battle with pride, however, was more of a sneak attack. In fact, my pride had been disguised behind my Christianity for some time. Of all the self-realizations throughout this process, this is the most humbling and embarrassing. I've come to believe that those of us who are saved at an early age, before falling into deep sin, are more susceptible to pride than others. A committed follower of Christ is less likely to be tempted by the lust of the flesh than by the pride of life (Genesis 3:6). The last piece of spiritual armor is in Ephesians 6:17, *"And take the helmet of salvation..."* Again, I love Warren Wiersbe's insights. He writes, "Satan wants to attack the mind...The helmet refers to the mind controlled by God. When God controls the mind, Satan cannot lead the believer astray."[7]

For years the enemy successfully used spiritual pride to create the misconceptions I had about myself. I never meant to be prideful. I just always felt that God was pouring buckets of blessings on me. Our family genuinely loved one another; we were happy. People actually envied my life because we seemed to have it all together. So many times, I remember thinking how fortunate I was to have the life I had. While gratitude is the right response, it is undeniably wrong to think I somehow avoided misfortune because of anything I was doing. Pride crept in and created the notion that my life was so blessed because I was special to God. I often felt sorry for families having problems. Of course, I soon found out how humbling it is to be the one pitied. Even though I was never actually untouchable or invincible, I no longer felt a hedge of protection around my family. Eventually, God taught me that trials and struggles are not necessarily products of failure, nor is a blessed life a sign of spiritual superiority.

Looking back, initially refusing counseling was also pride. I thought I could be the exception to the rule; that I could survive the unthinkable by drawing from my strength and my knowledge of Scripture. Notice the spiritual pride in my thinking; the strength and knowledge were mine. When people commented on how good I looked or how strong I was, it seemed to feed this line of thinking. Most of the people I came in contact with just never saw the continual turmoil below the surface. At the time, letting my doubt and anger show seemed like a poor testimony and disloyalty to God. Even asking others to pray for me was a struggle. This response to tragedy can be almost as detrimental to healing as total withdrawal from reality. Self-sufficiency was just another misconception. No person or family has the strength to endure such tragic situations in and of themselves. It didn't take long for my brave resolve to meet its match. My wise counselor kindly told me I was robbing people of the privilege of prayer by keeping my pain to myself. People genuinely wanted to help me and just didn't know how. Spiritual warfare is nearly impossible for a lone warrior. It requires humility to ask for help.

Reflecting on Spiritual Warfare

So, imagine emerging from a devastating storm, only to discover a war raging on your doorstep. Such was the aftermath of our tragedy. When the enemy attacked my family in June of 2011, I'm sure he thought it was a mortal blow. Surely we wouldn't serve God after He allowed such tragedy to take place. Although I did experience a set-back, reaching the bottom of my hope and trust, Satan did not have victory over me. The natural response to any victory is to relax. While this is a good time to stop and thank God for His guidance and protection, I must not inadvertently lay my armor to the side. The danger of attack can be highest just after victory. Even as this chapter is being written, the enemy is attacking my pride, doubt, and fear all over again. Each time God gives us victory, the enemy regroups and finds another way to come at us. So, even though I'd love to say my experience with spiritual warfare is over, the trials and tribulations of life are never a one and done rule. Unfortunately, I will battle the hurt and devastation of Courtney's death until I am laid to rest.

However, I've learned how critical spiritual armor is to my survival. As soldiers of Christ, we must keep our armor firmly in place. We must stay on guard and remain alert because the battle will rage until Christ returns. This reminder is not to discourage you in any way. Rather, it is meant to warn you against our common enemy and to encourage you in your own spiritual battles. Learn from the battles you have already faced. Then continue to fight, knowing that our heavenly Father will never leave you to fight alone.

Now, as I picture myself suiting up for battle, I realize the fight is not mine but the Lord's. The enemy will not win because my war was ultimately won on the Cross. Jesus is my Defender, my Captain, and my Victor. He's the One I follow into each subsequent battle. His strength is the key to living in victory on this side of eternity. *"But thanks [be] to God, which giveth us the victory through our Lord Jesus Christ"* (1 Corinthians 15:57).

Chapter 7:
Opening My Heart to Forgiveness

"Will you forgive me?" Four very powerful words that form a very powerful question. This question, asked in the right way and at the right time, can mend a heart or restore a relationship. Most of the hurts we experience are inadvertently done. Others are intentional. Either way, it's easier to forgive a person who is truly sorry for his or her offense. What if we never receive an apology? What if the person is not at all sorry for the hurt that's been caused? These thoughts and questions began to swirl in my head. It was a topic I had locked away in my mind. Even though my faith was beginning to strengthen, I still had so far to go; and withholding forgiveness was hindering my spiritual growth. Did I really need to forgive the person who took my daughter's life? The Lord knew that forgiving was my biggest issue at this point. So, in His wisdom and mercy, He re-opened my heart to forgiveness in a completely different place.

Forgiving Myself

Forgiving myself was complicated. Naturally, the bulk of my guilt was because we allowed Courtney to leave with that boy. I felt so irresponsible. To my mind, I was at equal fault and deserved punishment for somehow allowing her life to be taken. These harsh judgments on myself were a daily wrestling match during the year after Courtney's death. Because of the notoriety of the story, we knew people would draw their own conclusions; and there were those who judged us based on what they heard, read, or assumed. Of course, they weren't thinking or saying anything we had not already thought. And my thoughts were full of regret and self-accusation. If only we had asked more questions. Maybe then we would have known something wasn't right. If only I had said, "No!" and left the beach immediately. If only I could go back to that day and do it all differently; but I could not undo what happened no matter how desperately I wanted to do just that. It happened.

The truth is, there was no way we could have known this boy's heart or his plans. In spite of that, my mind couldn't accept this yet because I had not forgiven myself for every, "if only…." Once again, it was the truth of God's Word that spoke to my battered heart. One verse in particular stood out. *"And be ye kind one to another, tenderhearted, forgiving one another, even as God for Christ's sake hath forgiven you"* (Ephesians 4:32). Although I knew this verse well, I had never considered it in regard to forgiving myself. As I read those words, God helped me to see that I was the person in need of kindness and tenderness. So, I began to look at scriptural truths regarding forgiveness in a new light, applying them to forgiving myself. Several principles became clear.

First, forgiveness brings deliverance. *"Who hath delivered us from the power of darkness, and hath translated us into the kingdom of his* dear Son: *In whom we have redemption through his blood, even the forgiveness of sins:"* (Colossians 1:13-14). I understood this verse with full clarity. Divine forgiveness delivers us from sin's power. As a child, I experienced His deliverance, redemption, and forgiveness at salvation. But now feelings of guilt clouded my judgment. I still believed that Jesus› blood paid for even the most heinous sins imaginable, including the one that took Courtney. However, my failure to stop this evil felt like sin; and it seemed unforgivable. God began to show me, through His Word and His Holy Spirit, that these self-accusations were from a place of darkness, not of light. Remember the enemy's tactics – he is the accuser. Just as God's forgiveness delivered me from the power of darkness, forgiving myself would bring deliverance from this feeling of self-loathing.

Next, forgiveness is an act of grace. *"In whom we have redemption through his blood, the forgiveness of sins, according to the riches of his grace"* (Ephesians 1:7). Without a doubt, my sin debt was paid by God's grace. I just had no idea how to extend forgiving grace to myself. God's Word guided me through this difficult process. Colossians 3:13 says, *"Forbearing one another, and forgiving one another, if any man have a quarrel against any: even as Christ forgave you, so also do ye."* Part of my quarrel was with myself. In my thinking, I was both the offended and the offender. Again, my grief affected my thinking; and it became an obstacle to letting go of the grudge I held against myself. Just as in forgiving anyone else, self-forgiveness involved more than a simple change in thinking. To forgive requires action…a choice. Most importantly, forgiveness is a command. So, not only was forgiving myself okay, it was a matter of obedience. Even so, releasing those feelings of self-condemnation took immense measures of God's grace.

Finally, forgiveness is forever. Once we ask for God's forgiveness, He never throws those shortcomings back in our face. I love the way

Psalm 103:12 describes it, *"As far as the east is from the west, so far hath he removed our transgressions from us."* In order for my faith to be renewed, self-forgiveness had to be final. Revisiting any thoughts of "if-only" would surely lead back to self-condemnation. In time, He graciously helped me understand that it was not my fault, giving me the grace to love myself again. Of course, I still bear the scars of our choices that day. However, the pain I carry from the loss of my child is no longer an accusation of personal failure. Instead, those scars now represent my spiritual journey since the summer of 2011. They are reminders of how far the Lord has brought me, of how my faith has grown.

You see, what I viewed as failure, God used to display His mercy and grace to me. As He worked gently on my bruised and broken heart, I never felt condemned or forgotten, a fact for which I am eternally grateful. And He continues to give me the grace to face each day. He reminds me that I loved Courtney to the fullest extent – with all I could possibly give. But forgiving myself was just the first step; the next one proved to be even more complex.

Forgiving God?

Professional counseling helped me come to terms with many issues related to our tragedy. One of the biggest issues was confronting my feelings toward God. Because Courtney was taken from us so suddenly and brutally, her death felt like a betrayal of God's love. The hedge of protection I'd always felt around my life was no longer secure. Still, my upbringing kept me from admitting that I was angry with God. Even thinking it seemed disrespectful. To me, being angry with someone meant I needed to forgive that person; and the notion of a human being forgiving God sounded sacrilegious. After all, God did not owe me anything – least of all, an apology.

In order to avoid the topic altogether, I looked for other reasons why this tragedy might have occurred. None of them made sense in my mind. Even knowing that the enemy was ultimately to blame didn't calm my heart. My counselor was so compassionate. She patiently guided me through many intense conversations, finally bringing out my innermost feelings. I had no choice but to face the root of my problem...I was angry with God. For my faith and trust to be restored, did I need to forgive God? Answering this question is complicated. I had to really think about what it meant and what it implied.

In general, we think about forgiveness when we have been intentionally wronged. "Psychologists generally define forgiveness as a conscious, deliberate decision to release feelings of resentment or vengeance toward a person or group who has harmed you, regardless of whether they actually deserve your forgiveness."[8] It wasn't that I thought God had harmed me or my family. Neither did I think that He caused Courtney's death. God did not orchestrate those events. James 1:13 clearly says, *"God cannot be tempted with evil, neither tempteth He any man."* God did not bring evil into the world; people did. So, while we are sinners by nature, He is perfect. Sometimes, evil just collides with good. It is the way of fallen humanity. Yet, I was angry because He allowed this particular evil to happen; something I still have trouble comprehending. How could a God powerful enough to control the universe sit back and not stop this evil from happening? That question will never have a clear answer.

All of my questioning and searching for answers forced me to face my feelings toward God head-on. It was time to deal with the anger. So many times, people who experience overwhelming tragedy allow anger to simmer, which eventually turns to bitterness. It's especially heartbreaking when bitterness causes them to turn away from God altogether. So, I thought about the definition of forgiveness, "a conscious, deliberate decision to release feelings of resentment." And I knew Ephesians 4:31 instructed me to put away anger. Then it hit me...the real issue was with me. What I thought of as forgiving God was actually a matter of releasing my feelings of anger and resentment before they became bitterness. That idea reads so easily on the page, but actually doing it is more difficult than I can describe.

My counselor gave me a helpful exercise. Each day, I reminded myself that God is trustworthy by simply saying, "God is good" out loud. During the worst moments of spiritual warfare, I repeated this phrase constantly. At times, this was more of a forced statement than a proclamation of praise. I said it because I knew it to be true, even though my emotions tried to convince me otherwise. Some days, saying it out loud was the only way to keep from total despair. As I clung to God's goodness, I realized my misconceptions about Him. Until 2011, it was easy to say, "God is good" because I had a charmed life. When that was no longer the case, I became confused about who God is and how He works. My heavenly Father was suddenly an enigma. In order to release my anger toward God, I had to learn more about who He is and what His character looks like.

Suddenly, John 3:16 got my attention in a new way. How many times had I quoted, *"For God so loved the world...."* yet not truly understood the depth of those words? Long before my tragedy, God experienced the unfair death of His only child. He allowed the cruelty of the Cross to be carried out on His innocent Son because of His love for me. If He loved me enough to sacrifice His child, then certainly He would love me through the confusing emotions of losing mine. I was reading the most well-known verse in the Bible with new eyes. Its impact was like electric shock to my struggling heart. The deeper I dug into Scripture, the more of God's character I saw.

Jeremiah 29:11 has always been one of my favorite verses because it shows the Lord's heart towards those He loves. *"For I know the thoughts that I think toward you, saith the Lord, thoughts of peace, and not of evil, to give you an expected end."* Many of us, however, pull this verse out of context, claiming it as a promise that evil won't touch our lives if we're following God's path. Remember though, Jeremiah's message was delivered to God's people who were captives in Babylon due to their disobedience. So, the promise wasn't protection from suffering; it was His continual presence in their captivity. *"Then shall ye call upon me, and ye shall go and pray unto me, and I will hearken unto you. And ye shall seek me, and find me, when ye shall search for me with all your heart"* (Jeremiah 29:12-13). In the midst of Israel's enormous tragedy, God desired to impart His peace and to give them hope for the future. His character has not changed. He still desires for His children to know hope and peace by knowing Him; and I was more than willing to search for Him with all my heart. As I cried out to Him in complete honesty, my heart began to open up. I saw aspects of His goodness in promises such as, *"'I will never leave you nor forsake you.' So we may boldly say: 'The Lord is my helper; I will not fear. What can man do to me?'"* (Hebrews 13:5-6). Despite my tragedy, I could now make this claim with boldness.

One lesson has become crystal clear – we learn more about God in suffering than through times of comfort and ease. Anything He allows can be used for His glory. While this principle looks different for each individual, the most well-known example in Scripture is the life of Job. He was a godly and righteous man, a fact that the Lord pointed out to Satan. *"Have you considered my servant Job, that there is none like him on the earth, a blameless and upright man, one who fears God and shuns evil?"* (Job 1:8). Now, most of us would not volunteer as a litmus test against the enemy; nor would we feel worthy. Satan couldn't test Job's faith without God's permission and without following God's limitations (1:12; 2:6). Yes, the Lord knew Job would suffer greatly, but He also knew Job's heart completely. After losing everything and being struck with painful sores, Job still said, *"Shall we indeed accept good from God, and shall we not accept adversity? In all this Job did not sin with his lips"* (2:10).

Although I have told God on several occasions, "I am no Job," I also find odd comfort in his story. Like Job, my Creator knows my heart. He knows I wanted to give up, to lie down and never get up again. He also knows what I am capable of handling in His strength. Even though when I thought about living my best life, it never included suffering. Letting go of my anger meant learning to say with Job, *"Though He slay me, yet will I trust Him"* (13:15). I was slowly giving Him back the padlocked parts of my heart. It's hard to imagine where I'd be if I had given in to my resentment toward God. I finally stopped trying to make sense of it all and began accepting that God is good – no matter what is going on in my life. Moving forward, I stopped asking, "Why?" and started asking, "How?" How is God going to use me to glorify Him through this? And how will I learn to rest in His perfect character, allowing His peace to be my peace?

Yes, there are moments when my heart questions. I experience the pain of loss even now. I also experience peace that defies explanation. When my heart becomes restless, I think back to the principles I've learned about God's character, about His love for me on the Cross. That's when the Holy Spirit faithfully breathes peace over me once again.

Forgiving the Unforgivable

Typically, I listen to music in the car. However, on one particular day, about a year after Courtney's death, I was listening to a radio preacher. He was comparing forgiveness to uploading a file on a computer's hard drive. Once uploaded, that file can be shared with whoever needs it – now, or at any time in the future. The gist of his analogy was clear. Believers are to upload and share forgiveness. It doesn't matter if the person who wronged us chooses to download it or not. Storing forgiveness on the hard drive of my heart isn't actually for that person…it's for me. I was spellbound.

Now, I knew that forgiving the boy who murdered Courtney would eventually be necessary. Of course, I pushed those thoughts away as quickly as they came. While I wasn't bitter, my heart was definitely holding a grudge. I had even imagined various scenarios. For instance, what would I say if his family or members of the media were to approach me? Those conversations in my mind were anything but kind and not representative of how a Christian should respond. Early on I'd even written a letter to the judge, making my feelings about this boy very clear. When I read it later, I realized the full extent of my anger in those first weeks and months. And honestly, who would blame me? Most people would agree that my anger was more than justified. And because the murder trial had yet to be scheduled, dealing with my feelings about him didn't seem pressing…until that day in the car.

God had been working on my heart even before that day. After we lost Courtney, Christian music became a great source of peace in my life. Around this time, Matthew West released a popular song entitled "Forgiveness." It seemed to be playing almost every time I turned on the radio. So many of the lyrics were tailor made for me:

It's the opposite of how you feel
When the pain they caused is just too real
It takes everything you have just to say the word…
Forgiveness, Forgiveness
It flies in the face of all your pride
It moves away the mad inside

It's always anger's own worst enemy
Even when the jury and the judge
Say you gotta right to hold a grudge
It's the whisper in your ear saying "Set it free"

Then I learned the story behind the song. It was written about a woman whose daughter was killed by a drunk driver. Not only did this mother eventually forgive the driver, she was instrumental in his prison sentence being cut in half. Other members of the family followed her lead and also reached out to the driver in forgiveness. Subsequently, he accepted Christ as his Savior and began using his life in a positive way. One line in particular struck me each time I heard it. "The prisoner that it really frees is you." I guess I put those words aside because I simply wasn't ready to release my feelings toward that boy. After all, the drunk driver in the song was different than the boy who killed Courtney – wasn't he? The driver's actions were reckless and foolish, not premeditated.

However, something was different on this particular day in the car. I couldn't shake the thought that my wretchedness was the reason Jesus died. He was the sacrifice for the sins of the world – including mine. Yes, forgiveness comes at a price. So, did I not inadvertently murder Jesus? Who was I to categorize sin? Except for the grace of God, I too, would be headed to Hell. The Lord also reminded me of the promise associated with forgiveness in Matthew 6:14-15: *"For if ye forgive men their trespasses, your heavenly Father will also forgive you: But if ye forgive not men their trespasses, neither will your Father forgive your trespasses."* I have been forgiven of much. In return, the Father tells me to forgive much. But this much? Even though it boggled my mind, the principle was so clear in my situation. We had been greatly wronged. The person who took our daughter's life deserves punishment. While the law demands a penalty for the crime, the law of God also demands a penalty. I've been forgiven because Jesus took my punishment. Another line from "Forgiveness" says, "Help me now to give what You gave to me…Forgiveness." How could I withhold forgiveness when it had been freely and fully given to me?

The small tears that had been trickling down my face became a stream and then a flood. I remember the overwhelming urge to pull my car over, partly because the crying had blurred my vision but mostly because I was overcome. The truth from the radio preacher collided with the truth from the lyrics I could no longer ignore, "The prisoner that it really frees is you." When I began to honestly think about those words, my hardened heart softened. I realized with sudden clarity that the boy who took Courtney's life was not the only one in prison. By making myself the judge and jury, I had sentenced myself to life behind the bars of un-forgiveness. The key to unlocking the chains and setting myself free was within my grasp. By the time God called on me to forgive that boy, I had learned so much through forgiving myself and by releasing my anger toward God. I could not have started by forgiving him, which of course, the Lord knew. But now I knew the cost to my faith and to my well-being of withholding my forgiveness.

So there, on the side of the road, I lifted my voice to Heaven and asked the obvious question, "You're going to make me forgive him, aren't you?" The impression of the Holy Spirit was so clear that it might as well have been an audible answer, "Yes!" At that moment my only desire was to expunge the vile feelings of hate from my heart so that nothing stood between the Lord and myself. My anger toward this boy, though understandable, had prevented true healing. With God's strength, I forgave the greatest wrong ever done to me. To this day I cannot explain how it worked. The anger was gone, as was the intense urge for justice. Now, don't get me wrong – the law demands justice. It was just no longer my all-consuming thought. My contentment stopped revolving around his punishment. Although grieving Courtney's death will always be part of my life, the desire for revenge was replaced with God-given peace. God's love for us as individuals has always amazed me. He knows exactly how each of us best responds to His leading. He used a simple radio sermon and a powerful song to send a very clear message, driving me to the point of forgiveness.

Even though my heart had honestly "uploaded" that forgiveness, it would be tested because I couldn't forget what he had done. I wondered if I would retract my promise to forgive when we came face-to-face in a courtroom. What if he never showed remorse? And as far as I know, he never has. It's comforting to know that God doesn't require us to forget...just to forgive. He takes care of the rest. Of course, the resentful feelings resurface at times. When that happens, it helps me to remember how God forgives me: He does not bring my sin up again. This extension of grace enables me to refocus and release those hurts. The peace and calm I've experienced after finally letting go of the anger is the greatest result I could ever hope to attain. It really is like being released from prison.

The next step God impressed upon me was to pray for his salvation. After all, I had already taken the first step and it was a doozy. Even so, I didn't want him in Heaven where he would see my sweet daughter again. It was unthinkable for him to be anywhere near her, even in the perfection of Heaven. Praying along those lines was extremely difficult, yet God continued to work on my heart until forgiving him included a sincere concern for his eternal destiny. God's grace empowers me to earnestly and sincerely pray for this young man's salvation.

Beware of the Foxes

An anomaly strikes me as I finish this chapter. Sometimes the major hurts in life seem easier to forgive than the small, everyday hurts. Unresolved pain from the major strikes, such as a tragedy, can cause us to over-emphasize the frustrations of daily life. I've struggled with many of these smaller offenses since losing Courtney. Time after time my prayers have been interrupted by a bitter feeling or a thought that creeps in at an unguarded moment. In one of those moments I asked myself, "Why are these smaller hurts so difficult to overcome?" Then I read Song of Solomon 2:15: *"Take us the foxes, the little foxes, that spoil the vines: for our vines have tender grapes."* The underlying truth behind this almost lighthearted verse speaks volumes to me. Similar to the grapes in this verse, my heart was tender from the considerable work God had done there. After going through these steps of forgiveness, I was emotionally and physically spent. It also left me vulnerable in some ways. Often, those smaller hurts came in like little foxes, causing me to stumble in my resolve. This both discouraged and confused me. How could I forgive this major offense, yet struggle with the minor ones? Solomon's wise warning reminds me to strengthen and prepare my heart. If I want to be an effective servant for the cause of Christ, then I need to beware of life's little foxes.

Chapter 8:
Two Steps Forward, One Step Back

It had been a year and a half since that January night, sobbing inconsolably at Courtney's grave. During that time my faith was quietly strengthening. I continued with counseling and read everything about grieving my counselor suggested. We talked about the five major stages: denial, anger, bargaining, depression, and acceptance. She reminded me continually that there are no hard and fast rules to this process. Many people remain in one stage for years, some jump around, and others skip certain steps altogether. My family's grieving process was complicated by the fact that Courtney's life was taken. We lived each day, knowing we would relive it all during the trial, whenever that took place.

Something that affected me deeply during this period was the devotional book, *Women of the Bible*. We all know that Mary, Esther, and Ruth were great women of faith; but God also used Eve, a covenant-breaker; Sarah, a schemer; Rahab, a prostitute; and Martha, a workaholic. These examples are not in Scripture by accident. God uses imperfect people to accomplish His plans.[9] If He could use such flawed people, then certainly He could still work in and through me after my anger, doubt, and lack of faith - all of which felt like total failure. I learned that our Creator understands exactly how weak the human heart and mind are. The key now was to keep moving forward with God's guidance and in His strength.

So, that's what I did for the next six months. For the most part, I began to function like normal. My heart, though battered, was beating again. My faith, though weak, was alive. My family, though diminished, was surviving. The kids appeared to be adjusting, and I even smiled from time to time. Naïvely, I convinced myself that we had survived the worst of it. After all, nothing could be as horrible as the past two years – right?

After several postponements the trial was finally scheduled. Ironically, it was around the two-year anniversary of Courtney's death. At our request, the trial took place during summer in order to be less intrusive on the kids. We wanted them to have the option to attend the proceedings if they wanted to. It was important to us that their opinions and concerns were addressed. My new employer graciously told me to take as long as I needed. Cordy had the same assurance from his job.

As we prepared to leave, we were once again overwhelmed by the outpouring of love from our community. Friends volunteered to look after our home and pets, and we received enough gifts of food to last long after the trial. I guess I assumed people had forgotten about us after the initial show of support two years prior. Gratitude flooded my heart as the cards and gifts came pouring in. We were even offered a home in which to stay during the two weeks the trial was expected to last. During that time, these wonderful people actually lived in a camper to help make it as bearable as possible for us. God used all these precious souls to minister to us again, wrapping us in a cocoon of His grace and peace. No matter how bad it got, we knew He would never leave us without hope.

During those long 24 months, we had been in close contact with the prosecutor and many of the investigators. This communication resulted in lifelong friendships with some amazing human beings for whom we will always be grateful. Because we were so well-informed, we knew there was a tremendous amount of evidence against the perpetrator. We felt confident he would receive the maximum punishment allowed by Florida law – the death penalty. So, along with our parents, we traveled to Florida. Friends and extended family planned to join us as they were able. While we were scared to death, we were as prepared as anyone could be for such an occasion. I thought, "Let's knock this trial in the head and come home as victors." I had no idea that my forward momentum would be halted. We were about to take a step back.

The Trial

The first day was jury selection. We were instructed to remain at the house; they would notify us when we were needed in court. The prosecution team encouraged us to relax, but the selection took longer than expected. I almost wore a hole in the floor from nervous pacing. The call finally came. We needed to be at the courthouse for opening arguments that afternoon. The kids wanted to go too. Decisions about attending any other days could be made as we went along.

For privacy, we entered the courthouse from the back and waited in a little holding room. I was terrified. Cordy and I were both scheduled to testify after opening arguments. We had no idea how long or intense that would be. Really, we didn't know what to expect from the whole process. I remember being cold as we entered the courtroom. To this day I'm not sure if it was the actual temperature or my nerves – probably both. Along with both sets of parents, the four of us were seated just a few feet away from the defendant's table. Members of his family were seated a few rows ahead of us. The moment we had anticipated for two excruciating years had arrived. Although the forgiveness I experienced was real, I feared what my reaction might be now. Words cannot do justice to my emotions when he entered the courtroom. Cordy and I had only seen him one time in those two years at a pre-trial hearing. This time was surreal. There was no overwhelming anger; I was just numb. To be honest, my main concern was how my family would respond, especially Cordy and the grandfathers. We all made it through the initial shock and were ready to begin…or so we thought.

The prosecutor's opening argument lasted over an hour. It was brutal, especially brutal for the kids. He went into great detail about how Courtney died, using graphic illustrations and terms. We were hearing some of it for the first time. Knowing it was bad, we had intentionally avoided many of the details for our own sanity. I immediately questioned our decision allowing the kids to be present. Callie actually plugged her ears at one point, and Cole became so upset that Cordy had to leave with him for a while. When my father started moving forward in his seat, I knew exactly what he was thinking and feeling. Putting my hand on his knee, I asked him not to do anything crazy. At the outset, the judge had warned the court about outbursts or emotional displays. Daddy sat back and seemed to calm down a little. As detail after detail was revealed, my ears rang and my heart pounded. It was like some crazy horror story was being read…only it was reality – my reality.

Throughout the past two years, there had been moments of calm and peace. The routine of life helped us to compartmentalize. Naturally, we never forgot; we had just found ways to avoid dwelling on it. But that day it was as if we went back in time. Every tiny fraction of healing became a raw, gaping wound again.

Finally, the prosecutor concluded, and the defense team had their turn. Of course, they objected to the details being included and tried to paint the defendant as mistreated and disadvantaged. I knew they were doing their job, but in my mind, there was simply no defense for what he had done. The forgiveness blanketing my heart was in jeopardy of being revoked. My pain, as well as the pain of my entire family, was palpable. Many of the jury members wouldn't even look at us during those first days.

It was time for Cordy and me to testify. We were both asked general questions about how we became acquainted with the defendant and about the day Courtney walked off with him. Somehow, I avoided saying his name throughout my testimony. It was more for my sanity than to deny his existence. God again gave me the grace to endure one of the worst days of my life. That night, we returned to our safe haven both physically and emotionally exhausted. Two very long weeks lay ahead.

Day after day we re-lived the horror, enduring countless witness testimonies and listening to the parts we could stomach. For peace of mind, we opted not to be in the courtroom during the crime scene and autopsy portions and asked our families to respect our wishes. It just seemed to be the best decision for everyone – no matter how much they thought it might help bring closure. We were all painfully aware of what happened to Courtney. We didn't need images to go along with that knowledge. She had always been an intensely private girl. So, I felt that I was somehow protecting her privacy by not allowing anyone else to see more than was necessary. To this day, I have no regrets about protecting ourselves from at least that.

Encouraging calls and texts continued to come from home. Since reporters gave a daily synopsis of the proceedings, it wasn't necessary to share details. It was difficult enough to hear the details of Courtney's death, but realizing that practically everyone we knew was also hearing it was almost unbearable. Our lives were on display. Even though people were supportive, we were horrified by the invasion of privacy.

After a full week, the guilt phase of the trial came to an end. A guilty verdict seemed to be a forgone conclusion. After all, his defense attorney admitted his guilt during the closing arguments. Even so, we took nothing for granted. Along with the case information, we were also receiving a crash course in the legal system. Courtney's rights as a victim and our rights as her family were colliding with his rights as a defendant. We certainly wanted everything done correctly so there would be no legal loopholes leaving grounds for appeal. After the judge instructed the jury, they were released to deliberate. They reached a verdict in just two hours.

Our moment of justice had arrived. This storm had taken us to the depths of our pain and back again. We had come full-circle. There are moments in your life that stand out, moments that replay in your head like a movie reel. I had no idea how this moment, sitting on that cold courtroom bench, would stay with me. I think it always will. As the jury foreman handed the verdict to the judge, we held each other.

Guilty. Twelve individuals, who were strangers just one week before, came to a unanimous decision. Justice for Courtney rested in their hands, and they gave us all they possibly could. It was absolutely the only thing left that we could give our girl. Of course, it was the verdict we expected, and the verdict we had longed for over two torturous years. I'm not really sure what I expected to feel in that moment. There was relief, but no real sense of closure.

Now the penalty phase of the trial began, which ushered in a whole new level of anguish. During the next week, we listened as the defense painted a picture of this boy's damaged soul. His life was described as a "parade of horribles." One by one, doctors, specialists, experts, and family members talked about all this young man had endured.

The defense told the jury that he hadn't experienced a loving home environment like Courtney. He committed this horrible crime when his "tortured life" collided with her "enchanted life." Their argument, it seemed, was that his actions deserved a lesser punishment because he was so damaged. After everything we had heard over the past week, this rationalization angered me the most. My heart wanted to scream out during this process. Their entire argument seemed ridiculous!

And it appeared the jury wasn't swayed either. During the initial days of the trial, they avoided eye contact and actually seemed to be afraid of us. At some point, however, they began to look in our direction. While they had been told about our daughter's life, they knew little more than the horrible way it ended. So, before they made their penalty recommendation, we introduced them to the sweet and lovely girl we knew. It was difficult to describe this beautiful soul with words. After all, how do you verbalize your heart's dreams? We did the best we could by sharing pictures and memories. She was so much more than just a victim. I wanted them to see the impact her life had on everyone around her. I wanted them to feel the depth of the hole left in our lives without her. They needed to clearly understand that no matter what penalty he received, we were forever changed. Still, Courtney left us better for having known her, even for a short time. I've said on several occasions that she was too good for this evil world, and I believe that to this day. The old saying, "Our loss was Heaven's gain," though trite, says it best.

The jury left to decide on a recommendation for penalty: life without parole or death. Either way, he would be incarcerated for the remainder of his life. Of course, we were hoping for the maximum penalty. Again, the jury took only a short time to deliberate before returning with their unanimous recommendation – death. The judge would make the final determination at a later date, after another series of legal issues were handled. For now, we had received as much as we could possibly have hoped. Our long and arduous ordeal was over. We could finally breathe. I just wanted to go home, walk to my daughter's resting place, and let her know we had gotten justice. As we gathered our belongings and headed back to Georgia, we thought, "Now we can finally live again."

One Step Back

We naively believed that the trial, and especially the verdict, would give us peace of mind. I thought we would go home, resume our lives, and get some kind of closure. That did not happen. How does any parent get closure over the loss of a child? We would never get over losing Courtney. We could only try to move forward, which we longed to do. So, Cordy and I returned to work; and the kids tried their best to enjoy the remainder of summer. Although our wounds had been reopened by the trial, we felt that things would be better soon.

It took about four months for the judge to hand down his sentence. This time, Cordy and I went to Florida without family. The two of us felt strongly that this was something we needed to do alone. The judge agreed with the jury's recommendation and declared that Steven Cozzie would be put to death for his crimes against Courtney. The death penalty carried an automatic appeal. So even though the trial was officially over, we would have to wait years to see the sentence actually carried out. Somehow that didn't seem to be an issue at this point. After all, we had already been serving our life sentence for over two years; and it carried no chance of appeal. Then life took an unexpected turn after the sentencing.

From counseling, I knew that our grieving process could take longer than usual due to waiting for the trial. However, I was shocked to realize that most of it didn't really begin until this point. For us, the sentencing was the milestone event that a funeral is for many grieving families. The flurry of activity was followed by an extreme feeling of loneliness. All of the shock and awe experienced by our community had settled down by this point. After all, it had been well over two years since Courtney's death. Even as I write this, it sounds somewhat unfair. This community had been there for us throughout the entire ordeal. Their affection and compassion had been so immense that it was often difficult to measure. We knew we were not really alone; it just felt that way. I longed for someone, anyone, to take away my pain. I guess we relied on friends and family to somehow make this bearable. But no matter how much they cared, the hurt was so deep that only God could reach it. When the well-meaning attempts of friends and loved ones couldn't fix it, I became even more agitated.

There's no doubt that our constant grief and sadness hung in the air around us. How could it not? As a result, even some of our closest friends began to avoid us. We simply weren't fun anymore. Our whole world had shifted, putting us in survival mode. Most days, the amusements in life took a backseat to just staying busy, which helped to keep our pain manageable. Things that had been important to us before mattered very little. During this time, just waking up became arduous. So, we basically withdrew from the mainstream. Some friends continued to reach out and stuck with us every step of the way. Most, however, simply didn't know how to relate to us anymore. As people turned away, my loneliness became misplaced anger (although it was well hidden). I began talking with my counselor again just to make sure I wasn't losing my mind. I felt like a ticking bomb. She helped me realize that I was just beginning to experience the anger, despair, and frustration I thought I had avoided.

These were dark days. I wasn't content in my job, and I missed my friends. The spiritual warfare became intense again - very intense.

The enemy seemed to be constantly there – whispering lies and battling my faith. Even now, it's hard to admit some of the thoughts I was having. Some days I even told God, "I'm done; the devil can have me!" This was definitely a step backward. I could relate with Job's lowest moment, asking God why he was even born. So, when people commented on how well we were doing, I thought, "If you only knew." They talked about finding our new normal. I did not want a new normal; I wanted my life back! I longed for a feeling of normalcy instead of this constant uncertainty.

Then one day I was reading *Though I Walk Through the Valley* by Vance Havner. In talking about the "valley of the shadow of death" in Psalm 23, He points out that where there is a shadow, there must also be light.[10] God never ceases to amaze me. Even though I'd read that passage all of my life, He revealed a truth I had never thought about before. The only way out of this dark forest was to keep moving toward the light. Still, in my pain and grieving, my grip on my faith was slippery…at best. Looking back, I see that God was holding me and His grip was just fine!

Slowly, we began to realize that friends who turned away didn't mean to hurt us. I can't blame people for not being able to relate with us; we didn't know how to relate with ourselves! Some inevitable healing has taken place since those dark days. Of course, the full healing we long for won't be realized until eternity. Until then, life still hands us problems and frustrations; we're not unique in that. Sometimes, life is a series of two steps forward and one step back. As I face today's struggles, I choose to keep walking forward in the promise of John 16:33, *"These things I have spoken unto you, that in me ye might have peace. In the world ye shall have tribulation: but be of good cheer; I have overcome the world."* I've learned that faith only grows stronger through exercise, and exercise usually brings some kind of pain. The results, however, are well worth it.

Chapter 9:
When God is Silent

One thought began to echo in my mind, "What now?" What did my commitment to moving forward look like? I had an overwhelming desire to use all I'd learned to help someone else. At the time, sharing what I'd learned was the only way my tragedy and all the struggles that followed could be used for good. But how?

Then I got a call from my counselor, who was responsible for lining up speakers for the National Day of Prayer event in our community. She asked if I would be willing to say a few words. The thought of speaking openly about Courtney was nerve-wracking. Still, I agreed…reluctantly. When the day arrived, most everyone in the room knew who I was; so I only touched on our tragedy briefly. I talked about the power of intercessory prayer. I focused on thanking our community for faithfully praying for us. Their prayers had given us the strength to survive. This event helped me overcome my nervousness about speaking publicly, and it prepared me for what happened next.

A New Sense of Purpose

A few months later, a friend asked me to speak at the Christmas banquet at her church. God was presenting me with opportunities to encourage other believers through my testimony. For weeks I scribbled notes, trying to put my pain and my spiritual struggle into words. Because I was so nervous, I chose to go alone that night. I had even written out what I wanted to say word for word. When the time arrived, however, I suddenly felt unsure about what to say. But God was faithful. Walking to the podium, I felt His presence in a way I had never experienced before or since. I don't really remember what I said after my initial remarks. God had used the preparation process to sort my thoughts and saturate my mind with His Word. So, without my notes, the Holy Spirit calmed my nerves and guided me back through it naturally. He showed me exactly what to say and how to say it. As the words about God's love and goodness flowed from my lips, I found that I really believed them. Now, for someone who had struggled with the depth of her faith, this was a healing balm. And amazingly, I only cried a little. This night truly belonged to the Holy Spirit.

When I finished, many of the ladies told me they were touched by my story. In the days that followed people continued to tell me how much my words meant to them. What a glimmer of hope! If God could use my struggle to point other people to Him, then maybe I could move from simply surviving to actually thriving. The exhilaration from that night carried me for quite a while. A new sense of purpose came over me. Even though I continued to work, (catering events and serving on the local school board), speaking about my spiritual journey felt like my new calling.

This new sense of purpose intensified my discontentment with my job. Other things were changing too. Callie was about to graduate from high school and Cole started driving. As both children became more independent, the time felt right to look for employment more in line with my skills and abilities. So, confident that God had the perfect position waiting, I quit my job and lined up a few interviews.

Two boxes of personal belongings from work went into the back of my car. They contained everything from candles to work manuals to desk accessories. It seems almost comical now. Have box…will travel. I just knew one of these interviews was the one, the job God had already picked out for me. After a few weeks, the candles started to melt in the South Georgia heat, causing my car to smell like a mixture of cinnamon and lavender. As summer came to an end, my dear husband suggested that maybe we should move the boxes inside. I was upset as we removed them from the car. This meant there wasn't really a job waiting. To make matters worse, no new opportunities to speak were coming either. Did God really bring me this far only to set me aside?

A Period of Waiting

I wish I could tell you that I waited patiently and that my faith never wavered. Oh, it wavered! I even began to question God again. The feelings of usefulness and optimism from earlier in the year began to wane. As fall arrived and Callie left for college, boredom, loneliness, and worry settled in. Now, a lot of moms experience some level of anxiety when a child leaves for school. For me, this normal life event was exacerbated by the loss of another child. Despite the fact that she was adjusting well…I worried. How was she doing and did she need me? So, my phone was never out of my sight in case she called or texted. When she went out, I stayed awake until I knew she was safely back in her dorm room. Maybe I would have worried even if we hadn't lost Courtney so suddenly, but it was definitely on my mind most days. Then came the realization that it was just a matter of time before Cole left as well. My refrigerator that had once been covered with schedules and appointments for the kids was not as full as it had been. Callie and Cole were finding their own way, taking care of their own schedules. Although this was the natural progression of things, it hurt my heart and added to my restlessness.

Additionally, I was dealing with low self-esteem from each job opportunity ending with, "Thank you for applying, but...." One interview after another, I explained to God that I needed to be busy doing something important. As each month passed, I expected a position or a speaking engagement to open up; but nothing happened. God remained silent. During those days, I pictured myself as a clay jar. Just as a potter works with clay, God had worked in my life in remarkable ways. Since Courtney's death, He had shaped and re-shaped the thoughts and beliefs that previously defined me. Now my biggest fear was that He would put me on a shelf and leave me sitting there. How could I be a useful vessel by doing nothing?

I was eager to share what God had taught me in my spiritual journey; and in doing so, give Him the glory and honor He deserves. And yes, I was determined not to waste the pain and suffering of our loss. But in my eagerness and determination, I misunderstood God's silence. Just because I wasn't active didn't mean He wasn't. You see, I wasn't on the shelf at all; I was still on the potter's wheel! He was still shaping me, making me a fit vessel. This was a difficult concept to grasp, considering everything God had already done. Misconceptions were corrected; faith was restored; and forgiveness was bestowed. It was baffling to think that God was taking me further into the depths to refine me. Then Romans 8:28 came to mind once more, *"And we know that all things work together for good to them that love God, to them who are called according to His purpose."* This intense period of quiet waiting was working for my good. He knew I needed more time. In order to use my story as a witness, my spirit needed to be strong and healthy.

So, I prayed and waited. Which is, of course, exactly what the Lord wanted me to do. As time went on, I began to feel like the Prophet Elijah beside the brook Cherith. God knew His prophet was overwhelmed. After experiencing both great victory and great discouragement within a short period, Elijah needed time away to restore his perspective. So, God sent Elijah to the brook in order to minister to him. He provided for Elijah's needs, causing ravens to bring food every morning and every evening. What really spoke to me was the spiritual refreshing Elijah received. That's when I realized…this was my time by the brook. He was graciously giving me time to recuperate from the past few years. After all, it had been beyond exhausting.

When we first lost Courtney, extreme quiet weighed me down with fear and anxiety. I learned to embrace God's comfort in the quiet of this waiting period. Even though I still ached for Courtney, my heart was becoming more peaceful and my emotional wounds showed signs of healing. I began to hear God's *"still small voice"* in the simple things such as doing yard work and going for long walks. His whispers became more recognizable in the beauty of a bird's song or the blue sky – things I had to slow down to appreciate again.

Of course, what God was doing during this waiting period is glaringly obvious now. It's when I began this book. In the early days after losing Courtney, God started laying it on my heart to write all of this down. I shared that leading with very few people, talking with my mom the most. Because she knows me as only a mother can, she knew this waiting period was extremely difficult for me. One day, during an intense conversation, she encouraged me to take the first step…just start writing.

My beginning efforts were half-hearted, at best. Putting my intense pain and suffering into actual words was gut-wrenching. I relived each horrible moment. Those initial writing sessions took so much out of me that I had to stop for weeks at a time to regroup. But as I continued to write about God's comfort and grace, my heart started to quiet. I was healing without realizing it. Understanding began to dawn. God was using the writing process to clarify and hone my story in my own mind. It was overwhelming to see years of spiritual battles and the resulting growth in one place. Slowly, my impatience for God to act turned into calm anticipation.

Looking back, I'm amazed at how God provided during this period. I learned to rely on Him completely for every need – spiritual or otherwise. We went from two incomes to one at a very inopportune time. Yet, like Elijah, God was our faithful Provider; every need was met. We even had many of the things we wanted. Each month I thanked God for His provision and began praying for the next month. This period also provided an opportunity to show my young adult children what living by faith looks like, though I wish my example had been stronger. I think children learn a lot by watching how we get back up after we fall. And believe me, I was transparent! My kids saw the emotional toll of writing this book and expressed concern about my well-being. After discussing it, they saw the value in telling our story and approved my decision to write the book. They also knew how difficult looking for a new job had been. Each time I went to an interview, they cheered me on and prayed for me. And each time I didn't get the news I wanted, they encouraged me and lifted my spirits. Even their friends were praying for me. What a sweet gift this became!

From the beginning of this journey God knew exactly what I needed at each point along the way. When my loss was fresh and the pain was at its worst, He spoke loudly through the love and compassion of our family and friends. That kept me in His Word, where He continued to speak clearly, correcting my misconceptions. It would have been nearly impossible to hear God speak in a whisper during that time. Like many people dealing with some kind of tragedy, I had tried to stay busy. However, I learned a valuable lesson when God slowed me down and sent me to the brook. There's an incredible intimacy that comes with quietly trusting the Lord when it seems He's doing nothing.

This lesson was reinforced in my daily quiet time while reading *My Utmost for His Highest* by Oswald Chambers. In particular, his insights on John 11 really spoke to me. When Jesus received word from Mary and Martha that Lazarus was very sick, He waited two days before going to Bethany. During that time Lazarus died. These grieving sisters seemed to be greeted with the Lord's silence rather than His comfort. In fact, Martha was convinced that Lazarus would not have died if Jesus had acted immediately (v 21). Chambers says, "Has God trusted you with His silence – a silence that has great meaning? God's silences are actually His answers. Just think of those days of absolute silence in the home at Bethany! Is there anything comparable to those days in your life? Can God trust you like that, or are you still asking Him for a visible answer?"[11] Ouch. I was definitely looking for a specific answer – receiving relief from my discomfort rather than sincerely seeking God's will. Was I questioning God again because He had not responded the way I expected?

As I continued to read, I discovered this wonderful jewel from Chambers, "God's silence is the sign that He is bringing you into an even more wonderful understanding of Himself. A wonderful thing about God's silence is that His stillness is contagious – it gets into you, causing you to become perfectly confident so that you can honestly say, 'I know that God has heard me.' If Jesus Christ is bringing you into the understanding that prayer is for the glorifying of His Father, then He will give you the first sign of His intimacy – silence."[12] Wow! His words perfectly voiced what I was learning in my time by the brook. With each passing month I was learning to wait quietly in God's presence, confident that He was working for my good and for His glory. And I love the irony. God used an 80-year-old devotion on His silence to speak at full volume.

Moving Forward in God's Presence

After nearly a year of waiting, God began to open doors. While on a spring break getaway with Callie, I received a call, asking me to share my testimony with a large group of ladies. (This call also led to a friendship with a woman who has become a dear prayer partner. I call her my "kindred spirit" – like Anne and Diana in one of my favorite books, *Anne of Green Gables*.) The invitation to speak made my heart soar. Then almost immediately God opened the door for a job. Why did it surprise me? His ways are always perfect, and He is never late. God knew all along exactly which job I needed and when I needed it.

Although I didn't realize it at the time, God used this waiting period to do His greatest work in me yet. Through the silence, I learned to wait on His plan and His timing, to not move ahead without Him. And by the brook, I learned total reliance on His provision and a new level of trust that I had never experienced before. Of course, I see things more clearly now than I did then. When God didn't open doors right away, I wondered where He was and what He was doing. The enemy began to plant another lie in my thoughts: God doesn't care about your needs or what you want to do for Him. He simply doesn't care about you. But this time I was stronger, and I could hear God's voice more clearly.

So, to combat this lie, God took me to Romans 8:32, *"He that spared not his own Son, but delivered him up for us all, how shall he not with him also freely give us all things?"*

There's such beauty in Paul's reasoning. If God was willing to give up what cost Him the most – His Son as my sacrifice – then why would He withhold anything else I need? His concern and care for me are already cemented in that reality. God had not abandoned me.

So now, when doubt whispers in my ear, I remember that Christ knows me intimately, and the Father cares for me deeply. The proof of this is not in how I feel at any given moment. Nor is it in seeing God act in obvious ways. Even when my faith feels small and God's voice is difficult to hear, I can rest in the assurance that He will graciously supply every need because He's already given me Jesus.

Chapter 10:
Learning to Hope

Learning to trust God with this tragedy has been the greatest challenge of my life. He allowed my worst fear to become my reality. As a result, I've been taken to the end of myself and have emerged a different person. Throughout this process I could see glimmers of hope. As my faith grew and I learned to trust God unconditionally, those glimmers of hope became brighter. The word *hope* can convey different meanings. So, when I speak of hope, it's imperative that my meaning is clear.

Hope is generally understood to be a desire for a certain outcome. So, in secular terms hope is wishful thinking. In biblical terms, however, hope means to be sure of an outcome. It conveys trust. When God uses the word *hope*, it means certainty. The key difference in the definition is Jesus. That's why 1 Timothy 1:1 says, *"...the Lord Jesus Christ, our hope."* This spiritual journey had revealed my weak faith. Since faith and hope always go hand-in-hand, it makes sense that my hope wavered as well. Hebrews 11:1 is foundational to this concept, *"Now faith is the substance of things hoped for, the evidence of things not seen.*" Warren Wiersbe describes Hebrews 11:1 this way, "When a believer has faith, it is God's way of giving him confidence and assurance that what is promised will be experienced...He will keep His Word."[13]

The glimmers of hope I experienced throughout my journey were always accompanied by glimpses of the Savior. In each glimmer and glimpse, God graciously demonstrated that He had not, and would not, fail me. I had always hoped that nothing bad would happen to me or to my family. After tragedy struck, I hoped that we would somehow survive the storm. Slowly, my "hope so" faith shifted to a "know so" faith. I wish I could tell you that I live each day in the full assurance of godly hope. Truthfully, some days I struggle with treating hope as a feeling rather than viewing it as a promise of God. Then God reminds me that He will never leave me and that everything guaranteed in His Word is true – no matter what. There are several areas in my life where His abiding hope is quite evident.

The Hope of the Unseen

"For we are saved by hope: but hope that is seen is not hope: for what a man seeth, why doth he yet hope for? But if we hope for that we see not, then do we with patience wait for it" (Romans 8:24-25). It can be difficult to hope in the unseen when all we can see is our sorrow and suffering. Yet, for believers, hope is there even when we feel hopeless. On the night Courtney died, I sat on the balcony of our condo waiting for my family to arrive. God brought the hymn, "It Is Well with My Soul" to my mind. Not really knowing what else to do, I began to sing through my tears. Like the writer of this hymn, my whole world was in upheaval. Horatio Spafford experienced a horrific personal tragedy, losing all four of his daughters at sea. As he sailed across the Atlantic to be with his grieving wife, the ship came

to the place where his precious girls lost their lives. He penned this hymn in that moment.[14] What a testimony of faith! If he could write, "it is well with my soul" while experiencing that degree of pain, then I could sing it. All was not well with my heart, but I knew without a doubt that it was still "well with my soul." How I had the presence of mind to actually sing those words can only be explained by God's grace. This would later stand out as my first glimmer of hope after our tragedy. A dear friend gave me a wall plaque that says, "It is Well with My Soul." To this day it hangs on my bedroom wall as a reminder that hope was there all along.

The Hope of Salvation

"But I would not have you to be ignorant, brethren, concerning them which are asleep, that ye sorrow not, even as others which have no hope. For if we believe that Jesus died and rose again, even so them also which sleep in Jesus will God bring with him" (1 Thessalonians 4:13-14). While salvation offers hope on many levels, one in particular has a deeper meaning for me now. My confession of faith in Jesus guarantees my eternity in Heaven. My daddy used to say that even if I had been the only person on Earth, Jesus would have died for me. If that does not humble you and bring you to the foot of the Cross, then I do not know what will. This becomes even sweeter now that my daddy, who instilled so many of the foundations for my faith, has gone on to be with the Lord. I know with certainty that my father and my sweet daughter both accepted Christ as their Savior. I can rest in the promise that they are safely with the Lord and that I will see them again. That's why I don't grieve *"as others which have no hope."* Hebrews 10:23 says, *"Let us hold fast the profession of our faith without wavering; (for he is faithful that promised)."* It's interesting that the Greek word for faith in this verse is literally, "hope." So, my

profession of faith in Jesus - my salvation - is a sure hope based on God's faithfulness.

The Hope of God's Faithfulness

"It is of the Lord's mercies that we are not consumed, because his compassions fail not. They are new every morning: great is thy faithfulness" (Lamentations 3:22-23). As I sought comfort in God's Word, I began to find verses I hadn't noticed before. The phrase, "great is thy faithfulness" really stuck with me. How fitting that God reminded me of His faithfulness in a book named for weeping and mourning. This was exactly the nugget of truth I needed in the midst of my sadness. Even when I am not as faithful to Him as I desire to be, He is always faithful – every moment of every day. His mercy and compassion are fresh each morning, giving me the opportunity to renew my hope in Him alone. Of course, there were times when renewing my hope was more difficult than other times. So, God gently spoke comfort to my bruised heart, especially in the early days of this painful journey. He knows me so well that when I need a tangible reminder of His love, He sends it.

Very soon after Courtney's death, I realized that I thought of her each time I saw a bluebird. Maybe it's because "Somewhere Over the Rainbow" was played at her funeral. Or maybe it's because my mother always said that red birds remind her of how much God loves her. Either way, these beautiful reminders of Courtney brought peace and comfort. Then I started noticing bluebirds at odd times. Some days I would be in a moment of despair and one would just show up. Each time was like a whisper from my heavenly Father, reminding me that His hope is certain, that my girl is safe and happy with Him. I've talked to others who've gone through various tragedies and many of them refer to similar reminders through creation. For some it's a rainbow or a beautiful sunrise. The important thing is to not miss these whispers of affection. One day as I was leaving for work, I was escorted out of my driveway by about a dozen or so red birds and about the same number of bluebirds. Needless to say, I cried for the remainder of my drive. To this day I consider bluebirds a special gift because they point my focus back to God's mercy, compassion, and faithfulness.

The Hope of the Soul

"Which hope we have as an anchor of the soul, both sure and stedfast, and which entereth into that within the veil; whither the forerunner is for us entered, even Jesus..." (Hebrews 6:19-20a). The certainty of my hope in Jesus is the anchor for my soul. When life's storms rage and the waves toss me about, I remember that my anchor is steadfast. So, I can still sing, "It is well with my soul." And He's not just my hope; Jesus is the only true hope for the souls of the entire world. The followers of Jesus in the Bible learned about true hope and faith when their grief over his death turned to amazement after His resurrection. This resulted in a burning desire to share this hope. They told others what they had learned *about* Jesus as well as what they had learned *from* Him. This was not a half-hearted desire... they were all in! They had a passion that comes with a renewed fire. Likewise, when my faith shifted from "hope so" to "know so," I began to replace fear with fervor. Now, I'm filled with a passionate desire to share what I've learned with others. Isn't that what happens when we walk closely with Jesus? We learn that He is everything. He is the anchor holding us steady through the worst storms of life. It would be selfish to experience such intense fellowship with our Lord and then keep it to ourselves.

The Hope of the Future

"For I know the plans I have for you,' declares the Lord, 'plans to prosper you and not to harm you, plans to give you hope and a future" (Jeremiah 29:11). Thoughts about the future were especially hard because it was a future without Courtney. When I spent time in reflection, the blessings of the past stood at the forefront of my mind. We were always a close family, enjoying life to its fullest. I thought about times we had played and laughed together, like our family trips to places all around the country. We also made it a priority to worship and pray together. At the time of her death, Courtney and I were challenging each other to read through the Bible. We would laugh about how difficult some of the passages in the Old Testament were to comprehend. Those memories are among the sweetest.

Each time reality interrupted my reflection, it was a shock. Yet, these reflections served as a reminder that the trust we had built in one another was not swayed or damaged by our loss. In fact, it grew even stronger. I remembered how God had gently guided my steps; how even in the darkest moments, His peace had covered my spirit. As time progressed, I began to surrender the idea of having a perfect life. I had to let God instill a new hope for my future and for the future of my family. That's why Jeremiah 29:11 has become my life verse. God's blessing upon our lives did not end when tragedy struck. Neither did allowing this tragedy mean that God had broken a promise. It was crucial for me to understand the difference between hope in my expectations and hope in the Lord and His promises. Once that was settled in my heart, I could place my hope for the future exactly where it needed to be.

So, we took a vacation to Washington, D.C., the summer after Courtney died. It was difficult, surreal, and even forced at times. Still, we had fun. We started laughing again. One moment in particular stands out. On the way to Washington, we stopped at an old mill and walked around for a while. The weather was beautiful, and my heart felt light for a moment. When one of the kids made a funny comment, I laughed so hard that I cried. After the moment settled down, Callie commented that it was the first time she had heard me laugh in a very long time. As we continued toward our destination, we talked about trips we had taken over the years. We laughed at the antics of each child, including Courtney. Again, we were reminded that although Courtney was not with us physically, the memories made with her would always remain. This proved to be a real source of comfort.

We were typical Washington tourists, enjoying the sites we had always heard about. We went to museums and monuments and even visited the White House. We made memories that did not include Courtney, which was the hardest challenge. But it was also a step forward in our healing. We discovered that memories of Courtney could bring smiles, laughter, and comfort. What an unexpected gift! During that trip I saw a glimpse of our future - a future filled with hope. We were still a family, and God was still there at the center of our new normal.

Hope and the Fallen Tree

With my hope for the future restored, I looked forward to what God was going to do next. Five years went by. During that time, I continued to seek God, and He continued to heal my wounds. I began to experience hope on many levels. Although the scars were still deep and present, there was no longer a searing pain in my heart, and the moments of despair were fewer and farther between. God allowed me to share my renewed hope in my salvation and in His faithfulness – both privately and publicly. He sent opportunities for me to speak with groups of ladies about my journey of faith. My heart's true desire at this point was simply to be available. Moments of doubt tended to creep in regularly, even though my faith was growing by leaps. So, when my resolve showed weakness, I would remind myself that God has never failed me, and He never will. These moments of weakness were almost immediately redirected to biblical principles of hope that had become so real to me.

Cole was in his final year of high school and Callie was in her second year of college. This particular year, their schedules synced perfectly and fall break came at the same time. Since we had not taken a vacation for the past few years, we decided that a trip to the mountains would be the perfect family getaway. We picked Callie up from school and headed to our favorite spot...Gatlinburg, Tennessee. As we left home, Hurricane Matthew was meandering in the Atlantic and was headed right for our part of the country. Of course, we were somewhat concerned but our home was well inland and we were determined to go. As we drove toward the mountains we just relaxed and enjoyed the nice weather. We were having a blast. It's amazing to think about what God had done in the previous five years. Life was filled with possibility again. We actually felt joyful. After what we had experienced, that kind of joy was only possible through hope in God's faithfulness and by realizing how He had held us close for so long.

That joy, however, was challenged halfway through the trip. We kept up with the hurricane every day to see if it was indeed going to hit our area. On Saturday morning we called home to check in. The damage to our town was minimal, just not to our yard. Let me back up and say how much I love my home. Cordy and I have lived in this house since we were married in 1993. It's not fancy, but it's home. It looks like an old home-place, which has always made it special to me. We have farm land with ponds and lots of trees. One tree in particular was my favorite – a black walnut tree that was over 100 years old. It shaded a large portion of my yard and made a huge mess every fall with leaves and nuts. Still, I absolutely loved it. In my opinion, it was a big part of what made our home feel warm and welcoming.

Well, Hurricane Matthew picked up my lovely old tree by its roots. Miraculously, it fell in the opposite direction of the house and did no real damage other than making a mess. When we received the news of the fallen tree over the phone, I was crushed. And when I say crushed, I mean devastated. I mourned for that tree as if we had lost a loved one. I moaned and cried that our home would never be the same. Basically, I acted as if life was over. Now this seems so silly and sounds ridiculous, even to me. But that tree had been there when we started our life together. It was there through our children's lives – through Courtney's life. It was part of us. It just felt so final.

When looking back, I say sometimes that I survived the unthinkable but almost "got taken out" by a black walnut tree. All of the hope that had taken root in my life seemed to have been uprooted with my tree. On top of all we had overcome, this was just too much for my heart and mind to take in. Needless to say, the remainder of our trip to the mountains was no longer fun for me. My family somehow managed to pull me up from the brink of despair and we headed home.

When we arrived, I felt sick. It was as if an old friend was lying in the yard. My attitude was terrible. Not only did I disappoint myself, I'm sure God was unhappy with me as well. He had taught me so much while guiding me through that deep dark forest, and here I was feeling hopeless again. And if I'm completely honest, I was a little mad at God all over again for taking my tree. My kids laughed at me for acting like a spoiled brat, and I absolutely deserved it. After all, it was only a tree. As I walked around the yard, I slowly accepted the reality of the loss. My attitude and my hope began to recover. If I had learned anything in the previous five years, it's that life goes on regardless of unwanted circumstances. And so it did.

Cole had a rather routine doctor's appointment the next day. Allergy tests were being run to figure out why he had been breaking out in hives for the last few months. I was happy to be off from work, even if it was a trip to the doctor. I needed a chill day after the unpleasant ending to our vacation. Mostly, I just looked forward to spending some one-on-one time with Cole. After the testing we waited for the results and to let him rebound a little. When we stood up to make his next appointment, Cole began to feel lightheaded. Without warning, his eyes rolled back and he passed out, hitting his head hard when he fell. The sound was so loud when he hit the floor that the staff ran into the lobby to see what had happened. Cole was not responding; he was out cold. Everything seemed to be happening in slow motion. When the doctor couldn't get Cole to come around, he told the nurse to call an ambulance. I tried to pray, but I had a hard time forming thoughts because I began to feel faint myself. Once again, my hope was clouded by old fears, anxiety, and yes – a lack of faith.

Although Cole began to stir a little by the time we arrived at the emergency room, he still wasn't responding to questions. He didn't know who anyone was or what had happened. My father met us at the hospital, and Cordy was on his way from work. Daddy could always calm my nerves just with his presence. He immediately sensed my anxiety and prayed with me. Up to this point, I had remained relatively composed. That changed when they took Cole back for a scan. Of course, that prompted Daddy to continue praying with me. Cole was awake when he returned to the room, only now he was combative and yelling at everyone. That was not like my son at all.

In that moment, fear took a vice grip on my heart. I didn't dare voice exactly what I feared; it was too overwhelming. Those thoughts and feelings were very familiar. Being in crisis mode with one of my children took me back. Once again, I was face-to-face with the reality of the unknown, and my old "hope so" faith tried to make a comeback. My hope of the unseen was clouded by what I could see; and it was scaring me to death.

We were waiting to hear the results of the scan when Cordy arrived. Thankfully, Cole had calmed down a little and was resting; so Daddy went home after we promised to keep him posted. As we sat alone in the room with Cole, Cordy and I quietly talked about what had happened and discussed our concerns. We both tried to stay positive. Maybe because I was with my soul-mate or maybe just because of the quiet, my thin layer of bravery dissolved. I began to cry. I spoke the words I feared most, "I can't lose another one." Even though reason told me it was probably just a concussion, fear had been whispering, "It could be more than that!" God wrapped His arms around us as we began to pray. Hope swooped in like the cavalry for my worried heart. In one instant, the Holy Spirit flooded my mind with the multi-faceted blessings from our heavenly Father. I was reminded that Cole belongs to Jesus. He had the hope of salvation that comes from accepting Christ as Savior. Cole's future was already secured. The same hope for the future that had given me assurance on our first vacation without Courtney still applied. Godly hope doesn't depend on circumstances. It was present in this moment as well. So, no matter what the results of the scans were, hope would prevail.

Finally, the doctor came in and said the scan was clear. It was likely that Cole had passed out as a result of the allergy testing combined with the blood draw. The shock to his body just caused him to faint. Cole only had a concussion. God had protected him. He was beginning to wake up and asked why his head was hurting. He knew who we were and was much calmer. The doctors agreed that Cole could go home as long as we kept him under close observation.

That evening, as Cole slept, his momma did some serious praying. I felt that I had failed the first major test of my faith after losing Courtney. The enemy had once again found me in a weak moment and had taken advantage of my old fears. Yet failure would have been not turning to God at all. While the fear and anxiety had been real, so was the certainty of God's hope. As I prayed, praising God for His mercy and thanking Him for His protection, I also asked for forgiveness. Just a day before I had been distraught over a tree. I had questioned God for not sparing me from inconvenience. I didn't see that He was still teaching me what hope in Him really means. It's so easy to slide into "hope so" faith – even for a moment. I pray that He never stops teaching me to hope in Him alone.

Aside from an achy head, Cole was fine the next day. So, I decided to go on with a speaking engagement for a small women's group that night. It had been on my calendar for several months, and I hated the thought of backing out at the last minute. As we dealt with Cole's injury the day before, I reached out and asked that group of ladies to pray. Now that Cole seemed so much better, I was overcome with emotion. I was ashamed and felt utterly unqualified to speak about faith. Although the previous two days had been humbling, I knew God had forgiven me for my temporary set-back and wanted me to continue forward. I prayed to my Savior for strength and for clarity of mind.

Before leaving, I walked around the yard to clear my head and get some composure. Of course, the first thing I saw was my fallen tree. I acted like such a fool over that tree. Yet, it paled in comparison to what the outcome with Cole could have been. Then I noticed a bluebird sitting on one of the limbs of that monstrous tree. It felt like my heart would burst into song. That bluebird reminded me that my God is bigger than the troubles and trials of life. He's bigger than my biggest fears. Responding to Him in faith means I don't have to be overcome when problems arise. He will always come to my aid when I turn to Him.

As I drove to my speaking engagement, my spirit was renewed. Yes, I am an imperfect vessel, but that's exactly who God loves to use. He gets all the glory because talking about Courtney in my own strength would be utterly impossible. Our story has no power unless it points to Christ. God allowed me to go through the worst tragedy I could ever have imagined. Still, I learned to trust Him with this tragedy. I learned that my hope is not in this life. My hope is in Jesus alone. As long as my journey on earth continues, it will be a journey of faith, pointing others to hope in Him as well. Then one day my faith will become sight, and I'll embrace my Savior...and my sweet daughter.

Epilogue

Life continues to move on. I have good days and bad days – just as I imagine each of you do. My faith is stronger today than it has ever been. Yet moments of worry and doubt still come. Some days, I have to pray earnestly for peace and to surrender my thoughts to God. If I have learned any one thing, it is that times of intense pain and struggle help to grow my faith and my relationship with Him. Even in tragedy, we can choose to trust God and to remind ourselves that He is good.

The fact that we survived losing Courtney doesn't guarantee that we'll breeze through the remainder of life. Challenges, both small and great, will continue. As Cordy and I face those challenges, I know that we are truly blessed. Our children are young adults now and making their own way in the world. Callie is preparing for a career in the medical field as a physician's assistant. Cole is a junior in college, majoring in electrical engineering. I'm learning to take my hands off the wheel regarding their choices and their futures, which takes a lot of prayer and trust. Our parents are aging and experience health issues that are often life threatening.

In May of 2018, my beloved father lost his battle with cancer. We are comforted by the fact he is with the Lord, and we will see him again soon.

We also continue to follow the legal appeals for the man who took our daughter's life. Updated information comes several times a year, and each time we're taken back to the anguish we felt during the trial. This ongoing process could take years – a fact I've learned to accept. God never fails to encourage my heart each time a legal setback occurs.

Even though writing this book has been difficult at times, this story of grace and restoration needed to be told. I am neither unique nor special in my journey. You, too, can trust God with your tragedy. He loves you supremely and desires nothing but the very best for you. My prayer is that my story helps to heal the overwhelming pain in your life. Remember, you are never alone when you know the Savior. May God richly bless you.

End Notes

1. Billy Graham. "God is not the author of evil - Satan is." Posted July 12, 2016. *The Kansas City Star Online.* https://www.kansascity.com/living/liv-columns-blogs/billy-graham/article88879052.html

2. F.F. Bruce. *Hard Sayings of Jesus.* (Downers Grove, Illinois: InterVarsity Press, 1983), 93

3. Susan Pease Gadoua, L.C.S.W. "Can Marriage Survive When Your Child Dies Under Your Watch?" *Psychology Today Online.* Posted June 22, 2017. https://www.psychologytoday.com/us/blog/contemplating-divorce/201706/can-marriage-survive-when-your-child-dies-under-your-watch

4. Dr. Christina Hibbert. "Siblings & Grief." http://www.drchristinahibbert.com/dealing-with-grief/siblings-grief-10-things-everyone-should-know/

5. Gadoua. Ibid.

6. Warren W. Wiersbe. *The Bible Exposition Commentary: Volume 2.* (Wheaton, Illinois: Victor Books, 1989), 58.

7. Ibid., 58.

8. "What is Forgiveness?" *Greater Good Magazine Online.* https://greatergood.berkeley.edu/topic/forgiveness/definition

9. Jean Syswerda. *Women of the Bible.* (Zondervan, 2002).

10. Vance Havner. *Though I Walk Through the Valley.* (Shoals, Indiana: Kingsley Press, 2018), 12.

11. Oswald Chambers. *My Utmost for His Highest.* (New York: Oswald Chambers Publications Association, Ltd., 1963), 285.

12. Ibid.

13. Wiersbe, *The Bible Exposition Commentary: Volume 2,* 317-318.

14. "History of Hymns: 'It is Well with My Soul.'" Posted June 7, 2013. *Discipleship Ministries.* https://www.umcdiscipleship.org/resources/history-of-hymns-it-is-well-with-my-soul

CPSIA information can be obtained
at www.ICGtesting.com
Printed in the USA
FSHW022206231020

9 781939 283122